Reframe Your Blame

There is only one word to describe these concepts—"WOW!" My life has changed significantly since applying Personal Accountability. I now know that my boundaries are limitless.

Linda Herkert

Reframe Your Blame shows how Personal Accountability can change negative self-talk, disrespect, and low self-esteem into confidence, pride and respect of others. Based on my results, it works!

Ben Oakden

Practical Accountability put it all together for me and made it gel. The irrefutably logical and deceptively simple concepts are truly life-altering.

Dr. Brian Read

For me, this was a huge turning point. An amazing process, it has changed my life for the better.

Laura Halleran

Going through my journey of self-improvement/self-discovery, I really thought I was being personally accountable for all of the situations that were happening in my life. Through *Reframe Your Blame*, I have discovered that life does not have to be so painful and difficult. My relationships with others and, more importantly, myself have improved immensely! It is an invaluable process for creating the joy in my life that I have been searching for and deserve.

Brenda Walker

Reframe Your Blame

How to Be Personally Accountable

Jay Fiset

Personal Best Publications
Calgary

Proceeds from this book go to support the United Nations Millennium Project. For more information about this amazing project visit
www.unmillenniumproject.org

Personal Best Publications
1301 10th Avenue S.W.
Calgary, AB, T3C OJ4
Phone 403-269-2378
Toll Free 1-877-806-2378
www.personalbestseminars.com

Cover design by Angella Thompson
Back cover photo of Jay Fiset by Dr. Alan M. Chong

Fiset, Jay.
    Reframe your blame: how to be
    personally accountable.
    1. Fiset, Jay. 2. Accountability. 3. Motivational.

ISBN-10: 1-894346-00-9
ISBN-13: 978-1-894346-00-9

To my son Wyatt Zane Haruki Fiset,
a shining light in our lives.
Your Mom and I are honored to be your parents.

ACKNOWLEDGEMENTS

My gratitude, first to my Mom, Myrna Fiset, for asking "What do you think makes them act that way?" thus sparking my interest in what makes people tick.

And to Cory, my wife, my friend, and my partner of two decades. Our relationship has taught me the enormous joys of being personally accountable.

And to David Comte who was instrumental in creating the painful and traumatic experience that motivated me to write this book.

And to the many others who have played a significant role in the development of these concepts and the development of me.

Thank you.

Contents

FOREWORD

What No One Else Tells You

Most people think there is some "secret" or easy trick to life that everyone else knows all about, but they don't. The truth is, there *is*. The truth is also that the secret, although very easy to grasp, can take effort to master. That's why so few benefit from it.

This book intends to give you the foundation of what is implied or briefly stated in every personal development book. I'm going to show you how to create positive change in your life through *Personal Accountability*. My objective is to remove the mystery and provide specific steps and tools to support you so you can experience this amazing freedom in your life.

Use this book as a workbook and apply the ideas to your life. Do the activities. You will find ample space to note your thoughts and reactions. Please don't just read this book. Experience it.

My Motive for Writing This Book

Working in the personal development field for twenty years has been very rewarding. It has allowed me to fulfill my mission, which is to live passionately, positively, and abundantly; manifesting freedom through Personal Accountability in all areas of my life and encouraging it in the lives of others.

When I examined the patterns of people who successfully apply the concepts of consciousness and personal development, I discovered a powerful theme. Those who seemed to remain stuck in their lives appeared to have missed a vital concept or tool. As I researched and observed, it became clear to me that many people do not change or evolve because they don't understand or are not able to apply the vital foundation of Personal Accountability in all areas of life.

The Promises of Personal Accountability

The benefits and possibilities that are created by being personally accountable are countless. Personal Accountability is the prerequisite to *all* personal development and evolution. Here are just some of the more obvious rewards you will experience in your life if you choose to make being personally accountable your priority.

- You will become a generator of positive energy.
- You will be more present in your life and free to choose your responses consciously versus reacting based on fear and hurt.
- You will spend more time creating and living your life instead of creating excuses and avoiding consequences.
- Your capacity to risk will rise.
- You will become more resilient, able to cope with the ups and downs of life with greater ease and joy.
- The quality of your relationships will improve.
- You will be able to let go of the past, knowing that you made the best possible choices with the information you had.
- You will learn from your experiences, and your results in life will change. You will be able to stop the painful recurring patterns that limit you.
- You will be able to use the recurring victim experiences of your past to discover and consciously commit to your life mission.

There are many more, but I will let you discover them as we explore these ideas together.

PART 1

The Evolution of Personal Accountability

Why is this book important to *you?* Because there really is a secret to success, happiness and effectiveness. Every personal development book since the beginning of time refers to it, talks about it, and acknowledges its importance, but until now there has not been a book about how to live it—in simple English, how to be *personally accountable.*

Examples are everywhere. Anthony Robbins, in his first major book, *The Power Within*, included it in a chapter called "The 7 Lies of Success," dedicating all of four pages specifically to accountability. An age-old best seller, *Think and Grow Rich* by Napoleon Hill, alludes to it as one of the secrets of success, but never really spells out what accountability involves. In a more recent bestseller, *The Secrets of the Millionaire Mind*, T. Harv Eker lists being accountable as the "#1 wealth file." I agree with his rating in terms of the significance of the skill, but his remedy, which is just to stop complaining and blaming, is only the first step.

All human beings who try to change their lives have recognized that, "If it's to be, it's up to me." Yet, many people have great difficulty making the changes they say that they want. Why?

Why is it so hard to lose weight, create wealth, transform relationships, improve health? I believe that we have difficulty creating the results and experiences

3

we desire because we haven't yet learned the "lesson," the one vital concept which must precede all effective personal and skill development. That lesson is Personal Accountability.

The Two Opposites

Throughout this book, you're going to be juggling two opposing ways of dealing with your life. Let's define them.

Personal Accountability: A framing device that eliminates blame of self and others, providing the power of choice, participation, and co-creation of the experiences and results in our lives, real or imagined.

Victimization: A frame of reference, experience, or belief (real or imagined, internal or external) involving blame that removes or distances power, choice, and action. Consciously or unconsciously accepting and believing that you are a Victim.

We all have had victim experiences. They are an inherent part of any existence in a world where we control so little and confront so many forces that influence and affect us.

⌀ Consciousness Clue

It is not wrong to be victimized, and it is not right to be personally accountable. In many cases, you have every right to be victimized. However, you must ask yourself if this is your wisest choice.

Every one of us has had our heart broken, been picked on at school, been in an accident that the insurance company agreed was not our fault (more on this later), or been rejected by people who mattered. You are not alone.

And each of us has learned different ways to cope with these victim experiences, techniques like:

- Learning how to fight
- Flying under the radar (disappearing)
- Feigning indifference
- Creating drama
- Confronting obstacles
- Rescuing others
- Becoming righteous and arrogant
- Seeking sympathy
- Getting someone to save us
- Medicating
- Recreating similar experiences to maintain the uncomfortable comfort zone

The coping mechanisms are unlimited, although there are some significant and powerful themes that we will explore. If you are not currently clear about your primary coping mechanisms, you will be by the end of this book.

Most people's victim experiences seem to happen over and over, becoming a significant issue in their lives.

Consciousness Clue

Your recurring experiences of victimization are one of your best clues to your mission in life.

Recurring negative patterns are feedback that you are resisting something. The important question is what?

Think about it for a moment. What if those recurring painful experiences are actually important messages? My observation of people who seem to be stuck in their lives is that they aren't changing or growing because they don't understand or are not able to apply Personal Accountability to all areas of their lives.

Please note that I said *all* areas. The fascinating truth is that most people are personally accountable in *some* areas of their lives, the parts that are successful. However, they are victims in other areas, those that are not working. All of us have blind spots, areas where we are unwilling, unable, or simply unconscious of how to apply the power of Personal Accountability.

The Meaning of "Accountability"

Do you have negative associations with the term "accountability"? Does it somehow sound penalizing and restrictive?

On the contrary! It is one of the most liberating, exhilarating, and powerful experiences you can have! I believe that, on some level, you have always accepted the power of Personal Accountability, applied it, and reaped the rewards. Yet, right now in your life you have areas that are not going as well as you would like. For example:

- Your career is not as fulfilling as it could be.
- Your primary relationship is not as joyful and connected as it once was.
- Your finances are a nagging source of anxiety.

Practicing accountability will move you closer to your goals in each of the areas where you want better results and more meaningful and fulfilling experiences.

This book will help you recognize some of your blind spots and provide a workable structure and spe-

6

cific processes to support you as you let go of the weight of blame and victimization and move toward the freedom of choice and accountability.

The Meaning of "Blame"

To most people, "blame" is a legal concept at the foundation of our society—who pays when something goes wrong, who is arrested and why. This legal blame may or may not lead to a decision of responsibility or of guilt and the resulting subsequent consequences.

The other definition of blame—and the one we will be dealing with in this book—is the *psychological* one. We watch people being held responsible for the results of accidents, actions, and misdeeds, and we assume that, by logical extension, every less-than-positive result must somehow generate fault, reproach, guilt, culpability—in other words, *blame*. This blame can apply to others or we can blame ourselves. Self-blame might sound a lot like being accountable, but as you will soon see, it definitely is not. It's actually counter-productive to acquiring true Personal Accountability. It is another form of locking yourself in the Victim mode.

So, let's think of the legal system as dealing with *fault* and reserve the word *blame* for the feelings and energy it takes to consider someone responsible for any wrong or unfortunate occurrence that has happened.

My Own Victim Journey

The event in my life that sparked this book was the loss of the majority of my net worth in an investment that turned out to be a fraud. The amazing thing is not that this happened to me, but that it happened *twice!*

The first time was in my much younger years. I had a business partner who took care of the money.

Not in a good way. This resulted in my losing most of my net worth.

The amazing thing about our vast and wondrous universe is that *anything* can happen once. However, if it happens twice, I choose to believe this is a sign that there is something to learn. And if it happens three or more times, then, without a doubt, we are consciously or unconsciously co-creating that event.

So when, despite my conscious precautions, someone walked off with the vast majority of my net worth a second time, I chose to view it as a sign. I dedicated myself to learning what I had obviously been missing about Personal Accountability and to apply it consciously to my life. I decided to become a walking example of the freedom and power of Personal Accountability, and, by implication, to show that if I could do it, then everyone else could do it too. (You will hear more details of my second victim experience throughout the book.)

Behind every recurring victimization, there are powerful clues about what your life mission is. Right this instant your reading this book about Personal Accountability is assisting me in fulfilling my own mission.

Consciousness Clue

Being victimized is what happens to you. Becoming a Victim is how you respond.

Who Is a Victim?
Terrible, awful, and painful things happen in the world. Perhaps they have happened to you. It is an absolute certainty that sooner or later you will be victimized. This is not up for debate. I simply ask you to consider whether *remaining* a Victim afterward is your wisest choice.

Q: I am not a Victim…but I am not sure that I am really personally accountable. Can I be both? Or neither?

A: Yes, the states of victimization and Personal Accountability can exist at the same time. For example, I can be perfectly accountable about my physical activity and self-care routines and still be victimized in business dealings or social interactions.

Q: I've had some tough experiences (victimizations), but I don't go around whining and complaining and trying to get sympathy. Why am I a Victim?

A: Please understand that you don't need to be complaining and whining to be a Victim. You become a Victim when you blame yourself or others for some problem or error. Every time you see yourself as having no choice (or at least no choice you'd like), you make yourself a Victim. Everyone who feels stuck and powerless is a Victim.

In Part 2 of this book, we'll discuss the four types of victimization (real, imagined, external, and internal).

Consciousness Clue

You can have a real victim experience and not choose to be a Victim. It is also possible for there to be no victimization and still be a Victim.

9

What Is Personal Accountability?

The dictionary definition of "accountability" is being responsible to someone outside of ourselves. For our purposes, we will add the word "personal." This book is about "Personal Accountability," an entirely internal event that has nothing to do with anyone else. Remember, our definition is:

> **Personal Accountability:** A framing device that eliminates blame of self and others, providing the power of choice, participation, and co-creation of the experiences and results in our lives, real or imagined.

Personal Accountability has nothing to do with being held responsible by others for a particular result. It has nothing to do with consequences or rewards. It is simply a position we take as individuals that empowers and supports us, helping us to experience greater personal power in our lives. Personal Accountability is all about how you *choose* to frame or view the experiences and results in your life.

There are many distinctions between accountability and Personal Accountability that we will explore in greater detail. For now, remember that, for most people, "responsibility" has a connotation of blame attached. With "Personal Accountability," there is no blame of any external he, she, it, they, or them and definitely no blame of self. Personal Accountability takes the position that your life and your energy are far too precious to waste blaming yourself or anyone else.

As human beings we do *nothing* by accident. Furthermore, every activity has a payoff of some sort. Even victimization offers a payoff and a form of protection. It gives us an excuse—an excuse not to risk and not to be accountable for our lives. We give ourselves permission to create a set of beliefs such as "I am powerless/helpless," "the world is not safe," "I cannot succeed," "I am not smart/strong/whatever enough." The more willing you are to tell yourself the truth about your payoffs and protections, the more likely you are to let go of your Victim framing and become personally accountable.

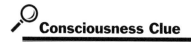

Consciousness Clue

Acceptance of the reality of victimization is a necessary prerequisite to Personal Accountability.

Activity – Benefits of Accountability

Write down a victim experience in your life. Describe how you felt about yourself physically, mentally, emotionally and spiritually.

Write down an experience where you were personally accountable. How did you feel about yourself physically, mentally, emotionally and spiritually?

Write down the specific results or benefits you believe you will receive in your life when you become more personally accountable. (For example, your recurring pattern of struggle with your business will disappear, you will forgive yourself for some past choice and will be willing to risk in relationships again, you will have the courage to stand up to someone and make yourself heard, you will drop your habitual excuses and take the risk you have been talking about for years.)

The Evolution of Personal Accountability

Personal Accountability: A framing device that eliminates blame of self and others, providing the power of choice, participation, and co-creation of the experiences and results in our lives, real or imagined.

NO BLAME

GENERATOR

Spiritual Accountability

I am a Spiritual Being having a human experience. My purpose here is to experience myself, remember who I am, and evolve at a spiritual level. I co-create everything based on this. I even choose my parents, and I choose the time, place, and method of my death through every choice I make in my entire life.

Practical Accountability

I co-create my results and experiences in life. I focus on my choices without blame. There is a lesson in everything, and I choose to find it.

Emotional-Response Accountability

I cannot always control or influence the events in my life, but I always have a choice about how I will feel about them. I respond without blame.

BLAME

DRAINER

Self-Righteous Victim

I cannot always control or influence the events in my life, but I always have choices about how I will feel about them and how I will respond. I can do this and still blame others, myself, the world, and circumstances for my life.

Self-Blame Victim

I made bad or stupid choices. My life is my fault. There is something wrong with me. I am powerless to influence my life, world, and future.

External-Blame Victim

Someone, something external to me, has done me wrong. If this had not happened, then my life would be better. They did it to me, and there is nothing I can do about it. I am powerless to influence my life, world, and future.

Victimization: A frame of reference, experience, or belief (real or imagined, internal or external) involving blame that removes or distances power, choice, and action. Consciously or unconsciously accepting and believing that you are a Victim.

There are six levels or stages in the evolution from Victim to Personal Accountability. Please take the time to read the chart on the opposite page. Study and familiarize yourself with these stages. It will make applying the concepts of the book much easier. We'll explore each of these in more detail and, more important, we'll learn the exact steps that are required to move up the chart and be personally accountable.

Activity – Growth and Evolution

When you have studied the chart, take a look at your life in general—the broad strokes and the fine details. Decide where you currently are in your growth and evolution—not where you'd like to be, but where you really are now. Write your answer in the space below.

Now look at your life more specifically. In what area of your life are you *most* often a Victim? In what life area are you *most* often personally accountable?

Perception Check: Often it is hard to see yourself accurately. Ask three people in your life to read the Evolution of Personal Accountability chart on page 14 and tell you honestly where they see you on the chart. What is their opinion about the life areas where you are most often a Victim? In what life area are you most often personally accountable?

The Three Forces

In large part, Personal Accountability is about learning how to consciously direct your thoughts and your creative energy to move you forward in your life. To do this, you must understand the three forces that create results and experiences:

- The forces you can control
- The forces you can influence
- The forces that affect you

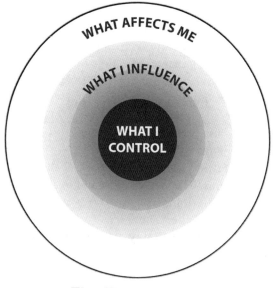

WHAT AFFECTS ME

WHAT I INFLUENCE

WHAT I CONTROL

The Three Forces

What Affects Me
Laws of physics, the price of commodities, others' choices and behaviors. Literally millions of forces.

What I Influence
Everything and everyone I come into contact with in varying degrees, based on relationships, interest, effort, and willingness of all involved.

What I Control
My thoughts, feelings, and actions.

The Forces You Control

The forces we control are the easiest to define and work with, though even here there is still some debate, misunderstanding, and confusion. The forces we control—the *only* forces we control—are:

- Our thoughts
- Our feelings
- Our actions

Most of us spend far too little time learning how to control these aspects of ourselves and far too much time vainly attempting to influence and manipulate the forces that are outside our control or influence.

I understand that controlling our thoughts, feelings, and actions seems out of reach to many people. In fact, an entire industry has grown up around self-help, personal development, and the science of psychology, because so few people know how to control their thoughts, feelings, and actions.

A significant part of the purpose of this book is to help you do this. The inner landscape of your thoughts and feelings determines what actions you will or will not take in your life. The greatest leaps in personal evolution and accountability will happen by focusing on and expanding the forces that you *can* control, not by wasting time and energy on what you can't control.

The Forces You Can Influence

There are a great number of forces in life that I influence, but have *no* direct control over. These include things like the output of my team; the enthusiasm of my audiences; and the behavior of the people I elect to political office, of my loved ones, and of my dog. The difficult part of working with the forces that I influence is knowing where the line is, what I can influence and what I cannot. The Serenity Prayer is in large part about developing the wisdom and discernment to know where that line of influence is.

The Serenity Prayer

God grant me the serenity to accept the things
I cannot change; courage to change the things
I can; and wisdom to know the difference.

Reinhold Niebuhr

A Story of Influence—or Lack Thereof

My dog Porsche is a perfect example. I can influence how Porsche behaves, but I cannot control all of her behaviors. With training and encouragement, I have been successful at influencing her not to jump on me and other people. I have been successful at house-training her. I have influenced her to sleep when my wife and I sleep and to do a multitude of tricks and behaviors that make her a wonderful dog.

What I have *not* been able to influence successfully is how she relates to and interacts with other dogs. She does not like other dogs and refuses to greet other dogs with the traditional mutual sniffing you know where. She expresses her displeasure in very clear and consistent patterns. Other dogs approach her in the off-leash park, and she informs them in the firmest terms that she is not interested. She turns to face them and lowers her rear end so that it is not available for the ceremonial sniff. Then she shows her teeth and emits a low growl. If the other dogs don't get the message and back off, she barks and chases them, though never biting them. As soon as they are at a respectful distance, she goes back to being her playful, trick-performing, loveable, fun, goofy dog-self. Until the next dog wants to sniff her butt.

19

We tried everything. We went to puppy school, super puppy school, and obedience training. We exposed her for hours on end to friends' friendly dogs and took her to the off-leash park every day to interact with other dogs. We hired dog trainers to come and work with us one on one. None of this changed her behavior. She does not want to interact with other dogs. I wonder sometimes if she thinks she is not a dog.

While we do have a great deal of influence over the behavior of our dogs (and children and employees), we obviously cannot control it.

Windows of Influence

This brings up an interesting related concept, the "optimal windows of opportunity" for influence. These exist in nearly all situations. Aware, educated, and conscientious individuals try to know and take advantage of these ideal opportunities. I suspect that our dog's aversion to other dogs was aggravated or even caused by our ignorance of a key development stage of puppies, the socialization period in the litter which occurs approximately between the ages of six to twelve weeks. This is when dogs learn how to deal with other dogs. We didn't know this when we went looking for a dog. We hadn't educated or prepared ourselves to care for a dog properly. After all, we were only looking.

But at our first stop, my wife, Cory, fell in love with this beautiful little puppy. The breeder assured us that the puppy was old enough to leave the litter and come home with us. Taking his word, we brought her home when she was a day shy of seven weeks old. So during her critical socialization period, she was sitting in our laps instead of playing with other dogs. Is it any wonder that she doesn't know how to interact with other dogs?

Think about results in your life when you have used a window of influence and it has supported the results and experiences that you wanted to achieve. Also consider the times when you missed the opportunity to influence and its outcome. I always smile when I hear parents talk about how, now that their kids are teenagers, it is time to lay down the law. A great idea, but about twelve years too late. The parents' window of opportunity to influence has already closed.

The job of teenagers is to rebel, define who they are, and move toward independence. This is a very difficult time for parents to try to begin influencing behavior. Only if the foundation of values and beliefs has been consistent from the beginning will the parents have an opportunity to support, participate, and guide their children through the teen years. If it hasn't, their odds of influencing will be slim at best.

So, the line between what we can influence and what we cannot is a moving target, based on timing, context, and knowledge.

The statement that "knowledge is power" is another way to say that the more we know, the greater our capacity to influence. Clearly if Cory and I had known about the vital stage of socialization development for puppies, we would never have removed Porsche from her litter so early. With this knowledge, we could have positively influenced her interactions with other dogs for the rest of her life. Ignorance is costly.

Still, the force of influence is a complicated area, full of grey patches. For example, is the intention of influence to support ("positive") or to manipulate ("negative")? How far do I push my influence? When am I guiding and when am I imposing my beliefs and values on other people? Each of us must answer these questions for ourselves, consistently and compatibly with our purpose.

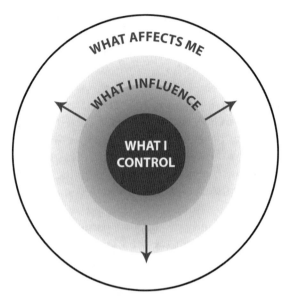

Where Do I Direct My Energy?

The Forces That Affect You

In our world, the countless forces that affect us are the largest area of our experience. The laws of physics and gravity, the turning of the earth, the heat of the sun, the weather, an accident, a natural disaster, the actions and choices of other people, the price of gas, the state of the economy—the list is endless.

What happens to us is important, but how we choose to cope with these forces is *more* important. Our *choices* are what affect our emotional states and well-being.

In dealing with the forces that affect you, the foundation of personal power is learning to tell the difference between what you influence and what you control.

The perfect way to reinforce powerlessness and helplessness is to focus your energy on things that affect you, but over which you have minimal or no influence. This wastes your precious life energy and creates victim experiences.

Activity – Your Strongest and Weakest Areas

If you are not actually going to do the Activities in this book, you might as well stop reading right now. Put the book on your bookshelf and prepare yourself to cope with your next victim experience in exactly the same way that you have in the past.

If you are still reading and you didn't complete the first Activity, Benefits of Accountability, on page 11, go back and do it now. It won't take long.

Now to *this* Activity. What is the life area that you decided you are most personally accountable for in the first Activity?

Is your energy directed toward what you control, what you influence, or what affects you? Write a line or two about what you notice.

What is the life area in which you decided you are most often victimized? Is your energy directed to what you control, to what you can influence, or to what affects you? Write a line or two about what you notice.

The Conscious Framing of a Life

Here is an example of the impact of living life at the different levels of victimization and Personal Accountability.

Recently Cory and I have been blessed to adopt our first child, our son Wyatt. We have chosen an open adoption because we want him to know that his adoption plan was made out of love, that his best interests were the motivation, and that he simply has more family to love him than most children do. (In an open adoption, there is complete disclosure of all information between the biological and adoptive parents, both parties choose one another, and contact is negotiated between the parties. That contact ranges from sending photos and letters to getting together for special events and more.)

We have just celebrated our first annual family-day gathering, having Wyatt's birth mother and birth grandmother over for brunch. At this point, we are in contact about twice a month. In truth, we did not adopt a baby. We adopted an entire extended family.

Cory and I have had many conversations about how Wyatt may choose to interpret his adoption. For example, we have a friend who, to this day, is victimized by his adoption—so much so that, when he and his wife were having difficulty conceiving, he would not consider adopting because he felt he would not be able to love an adopted child as much as a biological one. I do not pretend to understand that, but I did not live his life. All I can tell you is that it is real for him.

Wyatt, on the other hand, will have at least six choices about how he chooses to frame the event of his adoption. Let's consider them. (See *The Evolution of Personal Accountability* chart on page 14.)

Choice – External-Blame Victim

> Wyatt may say or think, "There is or was something wrong with my birth mother or she would not have given me up for adoption."

This framing will lead to a belief something like, "People hurt me and cannot be trusted." The long-term implications of such a belief are challenging at best—a life of being on guard, protected, and ultimately disconnected and lonely.

Choice – Self-Blame Victim

> Wyatt may say or think, "There is or was something wrong with *me*, which is why my birth mother gave me up for adoption. I was rejected because, for some reason, I am incomplete, not good enough, or some version of not worthy."

(NOTE: "Not worthy" is one of the most common core negative beliefs that exists in North American society. It is directly related to the experience of the Self-Blame Victim.)

If Wyatt chooses to frame his life at this level of victimization, his experience of life will be that of never measuring up. Whenever something doesn't go as well as hoped for, he will interpret this as his fault. He will be extraordinarily hard on himself. Over time, he will diminish his own self-confidence, self-respect, and self-esteem so much that he will be unable or unwilling to risk. Then, he will settle for a life far less than what he is capable of because he believes at a conscious or unconscious level that he deserves no better.

Choice – Self-Righteous Victim

Wyatt may say or think, "I understand that my birth mother made an adoption plan with my best interests in mind. I will do my best with the situation, but how a mother could reject her child is beyond me."

Notice that, at this level, he intellectually gets what happened, but there is still a wound of rejection and blame aimed at his birth mother. He will project this into every relationship he has, sabotaging what he intellectually knows to be true with the pain of perceived rejection and denial.

It must be obvious to you that if Wyatt or anyone else chooses to live life from the Victim frame, each new experience will bring more victimization, more rejection, and more separation. Over time, all Victims become "drainers." Drainers are people who consume more energy than they create, take more than they give, and ultimately have few or no relationships that work.

Yes, it is easy to see how these Victim interpretations could affect his life just as they could affect all our lives. Cory and I can't *control* how Wyatt chooses to see his life. However, we believe that we can *influence* his view with love, honesty, and openness so that he will choose to see his adoption experience from an *accountable* perspective as follows.

Choice – Emotional Response Accountability

Wyatt may say or think, "The simple fact is that my birth mother made an adoption plan for me. I will consciously choose to be thankful for my adoptive family as they are thankful for me. I choose to accept, share, and participate in life as it is, with love and appreciation, knowing my birth mother made the best possible choice she could at the time."

This accountable framing will support Wyatt to be present in his life; to develop an attitude of gratitude; to know that he was and is and always will be wanted, loved, supported, and the highlight of Cory's and my life.

Just this level of accountability will transform his life—as it could yours—but there is more.

Choice – Practical Accountability

Wyatt may say or think, "I have co-created the experience of having additional family (a birth family and an adoptive family), of being loved and cherished by even more people than most. I know there is a lesson in this about acceptance, love, and the definition of family, I will learn it and apply it in my life and with my own children."

Imagine for a moment what this would mean. Wyatt's energy is focused on who loves him and on the fabric of his unusually large family. The lesson is about applying love, redefining what family means, and deciding how he will give of himself to his family. What a marvelous supporting and empowering interpretation of an adoption experience.

Yet there is still one more step!

Choice – Spiritual Accountability

Wyatt may say or think, "As a spiritual being, I co-created coming here in human form to share my life and love in an unconventional way. In my transition from spirit to human form, I co-created healing the relationship between my birth mother and birth grandmother. Together, we chose the perfect family who love and accept us for who and what we are, divine sparks of God. We love and accept them on the same basis.

"I chose to come to the physical plane and have more parents than the norm, and to experience greater love, intimacy, connection, and contribution for all involved."

At this level of Personal Accountability, Wyatt believes that he chose both his sets of parents, that he participated, and that he did so with purpose. Clearly, this will lead to a life of purpose, one free of blame. This approach to life says that the event was not random or an accident. He will ask and answer the questions: What does it mean? What can I learn? How does it relate to my life mission?

Think for a moment about how Personal Accountability will impact Wyatt's life. And think also about how Personal Accountability will impact yours.

⚲ Consciousness Clue

The hallmark of Personal Accountability is absence of blame.

PART 2

The Victim Experience

In my coaching and seminars, I am often surprised at how resistant people are to the idea that they have been victimized. Now, I get that being victimized is not the most appealing of ideas, and that victimization is a source of significant pain in many lives. Yet, at the same time, it is so prevalent in our society that to deny the reality almost seems funny.

There are many ways to identify if you are acting and thinking like a Victim.

You are a Victim if you:

- Blame yourself or others
- Use "unaccountable language" like you, they, or them
- Feel powerless and choiceless
- Are stuck in resistance
- Engage in punishing, negative self-talk

There is another way to tell when someone has significant victimization issues. That's the emphatic declaration, "I am not a Victim!" followed by one of these statements:

- Because I don't go around whining about, _____ (insert type of victimization).
- Because I am a survivor, not a Victim.
- Because I don't blame others for my life.
- Because I set it up, so it was my own fault.

Of course, it can be difficult to admit that we have victimization experiences in our lives. For the most part, we want to perceive ourselves and have others perceive us as powerful, engaged, evolving, and growing, even if we are not. The truth is that we all have victim experiences. It's statistically impossible not to.

Let's repeat the definition of victimization.

Victimization: A frame of reference, experience or belief (real or imagined, internal or external) involving blame that removes or distances power, choice, and action.

There are different degrees of victimization— being picked on as a kid, not getting to do what we wanted to as teenagers, the many day-to-day situations that occur at work and in social situations, even serious accidents or crimes against us.

Denial of victim experiences is like a large neon sign on your forehead flashing VICTIM. It is similar to Emerson's statement, "Who you are speaks so loudly I can't hear what you're saying" or Shakespeare's line, "the lady doth protest too much." It is only when we are willing to see and accept that we have victim experiences just like everyone else that we can then move into Personal Accountability and begin to reclaim our personal power and our lives.

So, if you have made the bold statement, "I am not a Victim," I ask you to consider what is motivating that statement. It sounds like a brave, positive declaration, but in most cases, it is denial, judgment of self and others, or a way to continue to remove or distance your power of choice and action.

🔍 Consciousness Clue

We cannot learn from our victim experiences if our belief system frames the experiences as "these are about them, not me." Such framing allows us to dismiss the experiences and prevents our asking the deeper questions.

Can you accept that victimization is the reality of the human experience? Victimization is normal. It is inevitable in an existence where we have millions of forces that affect and influence us, but only three things that we get to control (our thoughts, feelings, and actions).

But just because victimization is normal doesn't mean that choosing to be a Victim is our wisest choice. Say the following statement aloud three times:

I have been victimized, I am victimized, and I will be victimized in the future.

How do you feel? Your reactions may include:

- "Yes, that feels true, and I resign myself to that reality."
- "Yes, that feels true, and I find the idea freeing."
- "It feels like it is probably true, but I don't like it."
- "I hate the idea. It was even hard to say it." Or "I refused to say it at all."

In my experience, the greater your resistance to this statement, the more stuck you are in your Victim experiences.

Acknowledge that victimization is neither good nor bad, right nor wrong. It just is. From this position, you are free to deal consciously with victimization, choosing whether or not to let it make you a Victim.

🔍 Consciousness Clue

Recurring negative patterns are feedback that
I am resisting something. The important question is what?

What You Resist Persists

One of the immutable laws of the universe is that you get more of whatever you focus on or give energy to. If you think hard about how you don't want to be victimized, you can actually attract victim experiences into your life!

Your brain or belief system doesn't hear or register the negative words like "don't." Try telling yourself, "Don't think of a red car." An image of a red car will flash in your mind. So, by saying, "I don't want any more victim experiences," you are actually giving victim experiences energy and you will attract more of them into your life.

Notice what you are resisting. This is the foundation of becoming more conscious in your life. (NOTE: If you have not read *Law of Attraction* by Michael Losier, I highly recommend it as one of the clearest and simplest explanations of how "what you resist persists" works.)

Societies Are Based on Victimization

Society teaches us to be victimized. We have been taught that deciding who is responsible is essential, and that, whatever goes wrong, there is someone somewhere to blame and even to sue. Our whole legal system is founded on this concept.

I challenge you to watch or listen to one complete newscast and not hear directly or indirectly that someone or something is to blame for the woes described.

There is a talk radio host in Calgary who regularly asks his woe-of-the-day guest, "Who is to blame for your problem?" or, even better, "Who can we blame?" Invariably, the Victim has a long list. To be fair, this same host also asks what can be done to fix the problem. However, usually much more time and energy is spent on directing blame than on resolving the issues.

Our society has become skilled in establishing blame (victimization), often from the moment of conception:

- She didn't take her pills.
- The condom broke.
- I couldn't interrupt the mood.
- She trapped me.

And, all too often, it continues from there. In fact, one could argue that blame and victimization have surrounded us virtually from the beginning of history.

Genesis 3:8–11

And they heard the voice of the Lord God walking in the garden in the cool of the day; and Adam and his wife hid themselves from the presence of the Lord God amongst the trees of the garden. And the Lord God called unto Adam, and said unto him, "Where art thou?" And he said, "I heard Thy voice in the garden, and I was afraid, because I was naked; and I hid myself." And He said, "Who told thee that thou wast naked? Hast thou eaten of the tree, whereof I commanded thee that thou shouldst not eat?"

This direct questioning by the Lord appears to have made our first parents very uneasy. Adam could have offered any number of reasons or excuses why he took the fruit. He could have said, "Gee, the sun was in my eyes, so I couldn't see what I was eating" Or possibly a modern-day Adam would offer this justification: "Sure I took a bite, but I didn't swallow."

What would *I* expect Adam to say—this man who walked and talked with God, someone who held the honored position of being the first human on earth? I wish he had said, "I was wrong. I'm sorry. I will never do it again."

Instead, listen to Adam's immediate response, "The woman thou gavest to be with me, *she* gave me of the tree." Adam is rationalizing his sinful behavior, trying to shift the responsibility to his wife, Eve. At this point, Eve has an opportunity to be a better human than Adam. However, her response to the same questioning is, "The serpent beguiled me, and I did eat." Pretty lame. The tendency of mortals to deny Personal Accountability seems to be evident from the very beginning.

Here is an interesting example of modern-day learning to blame. Close friends of ours have three kids. The middle child, Luke, is full of piss and vinegar like most boys. Luke loves skateboarding and gets a skateboard at the ripe old age of three. His Mom, however, is not quite as keen about the skateboard, because she is concerned that Luke will hurt himself. So she sits him down and talks to him about the dangers of skateboarding, reviews all of the safety equipment, and makes him promise to be careful. All is good up to this point. Then the inevitable happens.

Luke has a dirty wipeout and scrapes up his face. He doesn't cry and doesn't run to tell his Mom because he knows that she will be even *less* willing to let him continue skateboarding. But Mom has witnessed the wipeout. Later that day, Mom asks Luke what happened to his face. His answer floors her.

To cover up his skateboarding drama, Luke decides that it is better to say that his older sister hit him!

He has grown up in an honest and accountable household, yet, at age three, he has already figured out that blaming someone else for his mishaps can provide him with a payoff and a protection. In this case, it did not work, but it does often enough in general, and he was sure willing to try.

Activity – Learning to Blame

How did you learn to blame? What is your earliest recollection of blaming someone else? Were there any specific people or events that set up your patterns of blame?

CALVIN AND HOBBES *Bill Watterson*

Why Is Blame So Draining?

One of the truths about Victims is that they *drain*. They drain themselves, they drain their friends and families, and ultimately they drain the world. I believe that this truth is one of the reasons that people resist or deny that they are Victims. Most people would like the benefits of victimization without acknowledging the true price of being a Victim.

Drainers can be a giant pain, yet they are usually not malicious. Although they can act like energy vampires, for the most part they are simply people who have not yet learned how to get their own needs met. They cannot fulfill their own needs, and they cannot figure out how to get others to meet them for any length of time. Therefore, they try to suck up whatever energy, attention, and sympathy they can, in any way they can, trying to fill the void.

The saddest thing is that this just doesn't work. It is impossible for drainers to leach enough energy from others to fill up the hole inside them. Energy drains out almost as fast as it comes in. Some people in your life can't get enough, no matter what is given them. This will be true as long as they see themselves as Victims or, perhaps more accurately, as long as they see others or the world as perpetrators.

I had a woman training to be a coach in a certification program I designed called Jumpstart Coaching. Each coach-in-training must coach ten people through the Jumpstart process for their practicum. Most trainees quickly process ten people and end up turning away students because of the high demand. Yet, this one woman could not find more than three people in her entire sphere of influence who would commit to coaching with her as practice clients.

One part of this program is the process of creating agreement. As I worked with this woman, her stories of victimization and justification were astonishing. I asked her about the nature of her relationships. To summarize her responses, she said, "I feel like I have been giving and giving, but receiving little or nothing in return. So sometimes I just take what I want. That might be making people listen to me, putting myself in the spotlight, or however I can get their energy and attention."

I realized that the reason she could not create agreement for ten practice clients was that she had drained the people in her life of their willingness to support her and participate in her activities. She was trying to get her needs met in an indirect and unconscious way that distanced and damaged her relationships. It was not malicious, but it did cause pain. A fundamental truth about humanity is this: "Hurt people hurt people."

One last point about this example. How do you think she viewed her experience of not having any committed clients? You got it. It was all their fault. She was a classic External-Blame Victim. Clearly she did not complete the program and was never certified.

BLAME

DRAINER

Self-Righteous Victim

I cannot always control or influence the events in my life, but I always have choices about how I will feel about them and how I will respond. I can do this and still blame others, myself, the world, and circumstances for my life.

Self-Blame Victim

I made bad or stupid choices. My life is my fault. There is something wrong with me. I am powerless to influence my life, world, and future.

External-Blame Victim

Someone, something external to me, has done me wrong. If this had not happened, then my life would be better. They did it to me, and there is nothing I can do about it. I am powerless to influence my life, world, and future.

Victimization: A frame of reference, experience, or belief (real or imagined, internal or external) involving blame that removes or distances power, choice, and action. Consciously or unconsciously accepting and believing that you are a Victim.

To summarize, accept that everyone is victimized. To make sure that these victimizations are just events that we can clearly and consciously deal with rather than a habitual lifestyle, we must fully and completely understand the three levels of Victims—External-Blame Victim, Self-Blame Victim and Self-Righteous Victim—and how each applies to our lives.

Stop Reading Here If...

You may or may not have completed the previous activities. The truth is that most people don't actually do the work suggested. It is much easier to skim the contents, saying, "Yes, I agree with that," "Yes, I know that," "No, that is not true, I can't believe that." Some might say that this is "human nature," but I think that it is not so much human nature as it is a *Victim's* nature.

If you're just skimming, then you really don't have to do anything different in your life. You get to hang on to the excuses that make you feel safe. You can continue to be a Victim, maybe even contributing a Victim story to future editions of this book: "I bought this book to get over my Victim patterns, but nothing changed. All that money for a book that didn't work. What a rip-off!"

My point is this. You are coming up to a vital activity that will deepen your understanding of Personal Accountability and, most important, show you how to apply it to your life. If you are *not* going to do the next activity, then—again—I urge you to put this book down. If you are looking forward to experiencing the rest of your life as a Victim, replaying and recreating the same basic victimizations that you have been experiencing, stop reading now.

"Hmmm. Put the book down or do the work...put the book down or do the work..."

Still here? Okay, turn the page for your assignment.

Activity – Do You Accept?

Right now, you are either willing or unwilling to accept the reality of victimization in your life. Which of the following statements is closest to your current thinking?

- ❑ "Willing to accept" could mean I am honest with myself and am willing to face and deal with my victim experiences.

- ❑ "Willing to accept" could mean that I am victimized. I know I am victimized, and I have been stuck there for some time.

- ❑ "Unwilling to accept" could mean that I have been or am in denial. I do not want to acknowledge that I have been or am victimized.

- ❑ "Unwilling to accept" could mean that I don't believe that I am victimized. I dealt with it, and it's over. Victims are weak. I am not weak.

If you are still with me, then I am going to assume that you are willing to do the work necessary to transform your life. If you have not completed the previous Activities, *go back and do them now*. They will provide context for the upcoming activities.

My Own Victim Story

Before we move on to the really interesting stuff of victimization, *your* Victim stories, I'm going to tell you one of mine. Remember I told you how a trusted business partner cleaned me out when I was young? And how I resolved to avoid this disaster in the future?

So—a multimillionaire grad of my seminars gives me an investment tip. He had been investing with a commodities and futures trader whose trading partnership, called Titan, had been earning in excess of 125% a year. Now, *you* know and *I* know that "Anything too good to be true is too good to be true." However, my wife and I decided to interview the trader and his wife. We looked carefully at our grad's financial reports and statements. Everything checked out. Ultimately, we decided to test this unknown system and process by investing the minimum allowed, $5,000 US.

The Titan fund had been in existence for a year and half prior to our investment, and it continued its phenomenal performance, so much so that after about four months we invested another $50,000 US. We managed our risk very diligently. The partnership agreement said that if ever the trader lost 50 percent or more of the capital, the fund would be dissolved and the remaining capital returned to the partners.

So, while we reinvested our profit in other ventures, we also continued to invest additional cash into the fund. We were thrilled at the continued exceptional performance of the fund over the next two years. It was so consistent that we decided to put a high-ratio, high-interest second mortgage on our building, pulling out virtually all of our equity, so we could invest more money in the fund. (I can hear you groaning. You know I wouldn't be telling you this story if it had a happy ending.)

My wife, Cory, and I began making big plans based on our good fortune and financial success. We decided that we were going to change our lives. One of our many plans was to sell Personal Best Seminars in Calgary and buy beachfront land in Baja, Mexico. There, we would build a retreat and training facility to train and certify coaches and facilitators. Another plan was to start a family.

In November 2004, our account was in excess of $500,000 US and we had over $400,000 CDN in retained earnings on our company books. Then we were notified that the trader was closing the partnership. This was disappointing, but he assured us that he would start another partnership with the big players—and we would be one of them.

So, I did my best to support the trader, to make the transition of closing this partnership easy, and not to be a pain in the ass in the process. I was just so thankful to be one of the lucky few who could continue to participate. This translates to the fact that I did not ask to get my money out immediately.

Then, on December 16, I got the call. My sister asked if I had read the obituaries in the morning newspaper.

"No," I said.

She told me that the trader, the man holding our $500,000 US, had died. A few calls to other investors and associates revealed the terrible truth. He had killed himself.

I suspected the worst for our investment, and it turned out to be true. The whole thing was a fraud, a Ponzi scheme. The man had not traded for over three years. All the monthly statements were manufactured fantasy. And not only were we out the money we had in the fund, but also the retained earnings in my own company, plus we were on the hook for an expensive second mortgage. In one day, my net worth took a million-dollar loss.

To make matters much worse, when I was sure the fund was above board and legit, I had advised my friends, family, and staff to invest, purchasing in my name because it was a closed partnership. At the time, I believed that I was doing them a monumental favor. I was not supposed to do this, and based on the partnership agreement, I could be removed for having phantom investors. However, it seemed like a win/win to include others. They got the benefit of the stellar returns, the trader got the benefit of additional trading capital, and I was willing to take on the in-between paperwork to contribute to the financial well-being of people I cared about.

Clearly, it did not work out that way. Those who trusted me lost their money, and I felt awful. And the plans my wife and I had made, the land in Mexico, the retreat center, all our goals and dreams came to a screeching halt. We were in debt, our most significant asset had disappeared, and we had choices to make. Go bankrupt? Go to work for someone else? Sue someone? Liquidate assets? What were we going to do?

Of course, the investors were not the only victims. We lost only money. The trader's wife and family were devastated by his death. And he himself was a Victim because he had gotten in over his head and couldn't see a way out. (Real conmen who carry out Ponzi schemes don't kill themselves. They take off for the Cayman Islands with a suitcase full of cash and perhaps a blonde companion.) So a lot of victimization went on, and the survivors were left with the choice of using this experience or being a Victim.

Activity – *Your* Victim Story

Now it's your turn. Write down your most significant Victim story. Include all the details about how the person or people did it to you. Describe the results and implications. How did you feel? What did you have to do? What couldn't you do? Be honest. Don't leave anything out. This activity will be the foundation for applying all the concepts in this book and ultimately the foundation of your future life.

If you have already been working in your life to become personally accountable for this event or experience, I ask you to set that aside for the time being. Just let yourself dwell on the Victim experience. Take as much time and space as you need to write. Here are some blank pages for you to write your Victim story.

Your Victim Story

Your Victim Story – continued

The Three Levels of Victimization

Let's review:

BLAME

Self-Righteous Victim

I cannot always control or influence the events in my life, but I always have choices about how I will feel about them and how I will respond. I can do this and still blame others, myself, the world, and circumstances for my life.

Self-Blame Victim

I made bad or stupid choices. My life is my fault. There is something wrong with me. I am powerless to influence my life, world, and future.

External-Blame Victim

Someone, something external to me, has done me wrong. If this had not happened, then my life would be better. They did it to me, and there is nothing I can do about it. I am powerless to influence my life, world, and future.

DRAINER

Victimization: A frame of reference, experience, or belief (real or imagined, internal or external) involving blame that removes or distances power, choice, and action. Consciously or unconsciously accepting and believing that you are a Victim.

Each offers a course of action, blaming others or yourself or both. Each also reminds us that, when we are living without accountability, we are draining energy from ourselves, others, and the world.

Note that the descriptions of each level are clearly exaggerated to make the point and emphasize the distinctions between them. Usually, the experience is far more subtle.

Now, let's examine each of the elements of victimization in detail so you can see how they play out in your life.

Blaming Others (External-Blame)

Let's start with the concept of blame in general. The definition of blame is: To consider somebody to be responsible for something wrong or unfortunate that has happened.

One of the vital and obvious elements of External-Blame victimization is that we make ourselves powerless. Each time and in every circumstance where we blame others, we are reinforcing or getting to be right about some belief or set of beliefs that is centered on our being helpless.

I know a woman who spent a large portion of her life with an unfaithful husband. She was unhappy, but she chose to stay because of the kids and his financial support. Her focus for years was on what her husband was doing wrong. As long as she could vilify him, she did not have to take action. She was powerless to do anything, she reasoned, because she and the kids couldn't survive without him. She spent nearly thirty years hurting because he was unwilling or unable to commit to the relationship.

Ultimately the marriage came apart, and she was on her own. Do you want to guess what she did then? Yes—she chose to be in a relationship with a married man who, again, could not or would not commit completely to her and their relationship. Being a Victim was comfortable and familiar, allowing her to blame others and not be accountable for her own actions.

To check your level of External-Blame, ask yourself, "Who do I blame and for what?" Some people have an immediate list of answers. Typical are:

- My parents for how they did or did not raise me
- The person who abused me
- The teacher who said I was stupid

- The friend or lover who betrayed me
- The government, taxes, war, health care...
- The education system
- My wife/husband for not supporting my dream or holding up their end of the deal
- My family for rejecting or denying me

These are all classic examples of "See—it is their fault!" External-Blame victimization.

⌕ Consciousness Clue

If you want to become more conscious of when you are blaming others, notice when you use the word "Why"—"Why do they treat me that way?" "Why does my boss always give me the worst jobs?" "Why" often assumes that others are wrong and implies blame.

People who blame others are focusing on what affects *them* and what they have little influence over. By concentrating on these external elements, they prove to themselves that there is absolutely nothing they can do. They are, in fact, powerless, so they get to stay victimized with great excuses and tons of proof.

Language Cues for External-Blame Victims:

- I have to.
- They made me.
- I can't because...
- I tried that, and it didn't work because...
- I would like to, but...
- Those bastards!

Activity – Whose Fault?

Whom in your life (external to you, past or present) are you blaming and specifically for what?

Self-Blame

The next type of blame is more interesting. There are so many ways we can come up with to blame ourselves. Sometimes we actually express our Self-Blame aloud:

- Boy, did I make a stupid choice.
- I should have…
- I never should have done that.
- What could I have been thinking?
- It is *my* fault that
  - my relationships never last.
  - we are poor.
  - I never get promoted.
  - my kids are doing poorly in school.
  - we live beyond our means.
  - my spouse is unhappy.

More often than the outright statement, "It was all my fault," we use a more subtle Self-Blame, one we need to be aware of. It can be what appears to be a simple statement of fact, or it can be Self-Blame veiled by a story of poor or negative results. However, underneath the story or statement are Self-Blame and an excuse not to risk and move forward in life.

The experience of powerlessness is generated both by present events and by present events that trigger memories of past helplessness. A past event is re-created and projected on the present and the future.

Abuse is a prime example, generating versions of "I cannot trust anyone. People hurt me. If I let people get close to me, they will take advantage of me." The actual experience of victimization, in many cases, ended years ago. Yet, by using "abuse recall," victims often recreate the same or similar experiences their entire lives.

A participant in one of my seminars stood up in tears, saying that the meaning of the statement "I married my father" had finally clicked. Her father repeatedly told her that she was stupid and not capable of anything beyond cleaning house. Forty-five years later, she realized that her husband, while not as directly abusive as her father, had been saying the same things to her since before they were married.

Many of us are unaware of patterns of Self-Blame that profoundly affect our lives. Let's say that you truly believe you are in an accepting space and that in fact there is no blame attached to you. You may be right. You may also be harboring Self-Blame at an unconscious level.

◯ Consciousness Clue

If you are certain you aren't indulging in Self-Blame about an event, check the accuracy of your belief. When you describe the event, is there a twist in your stomach? Does your body or head slump down? Do you feel less powerful and competent? Examine the role that the event plays in your life. Do you use it to provide an excuse not to risk or not to be accountable?

What Self-Blame Costs

Notice that, in the following (true) story, I don't seem to be engaging in a whole lot of Self-Blame. I tell it entirely in neutral terms. Read it, and then we'll analyze it.

When I was in school, I was pretty good at track and field, and I was able to compete in both short and long distances. At one event, I was the anchor for our 4 x 100-meter relay. As my running mate got closer to me, we were in second place, and I was certain that I could overtake the first place team's anchor. I started to run. I felt the baton in my hand. I kicked into high speed—and the baton disappeared. I looked down and saw it bouncing all over the track. By the time I picked it up, we were in last place, and we ultimately finished in third.

For most of my life, I've been able to tell this story in neutral terms. Don't get me wrong. At the time it happened, I beat myself up for weeks afterward. But far more significant was the effect I let this incident have on my life. Because that was the last time I ran in competition. The Self-Blame that I attached to my error unconsciously stopped me from ever competing in track and field again.

Let's analyze another statement of fact that has underlying Self-Blame.

My business is failing, I have done everything I know how to do, and nothing is working.

Again, this statement seems pretty neutral on the surface. At first glance, it is a statement of fact. However, let's notice several clues:

"*My* business is failing." Not *the* business is failing. The framing is very personal.

"*I* have done everything *I* know how to do." Again, very personal framing.

"*Nothing* is working." This is classic Victim framing. Something somewhere is always working to some degree, but when we are busy blaming ourselves, it can be hard to see.

One of the easiest ways to notice our Self-Blame tendencies is to become more conscious of our negative self-talk. Behind all self-diminishing self-talk, internal and external, there is an element of Self-Blame.

I failed before.

I am not smart enough.

I am not strong enough.

I am not tall (thin, pretty, witty, whatever) enough.

I don't know how.

I am not capable.

Somehow, there is just something wrong with me.

I don't fit in; I am not normal.

I am powerless.

There is nothing I can do.

I am too confused; I don't understand.

I messed up.

The clearer you are about who, what, when, and how you blame, the easier it will be to understand and ultimately stop your patterns of being a Victim.

Activity – Self-Blame Stories

Where in your life do you have stories that, on the surface, do not seem to have blame attached, but the event significantly influenced what you would or would not do in the future?

Can you make a list of seemingly neutral events that you actually blame yourself for?

Self-Righteous Blame

As we move through the chart, our victimization becomes more and more sophisticated. We are still framing our lives and experiences from the Victim reference, but we are not so blatantly and obviously pointing our fingers at others or ourselves.

Self-Righteous Victim

I cannot always control or influence the events in my life, but I always have choices about how I will feel about them and how I will respond. I can do this and still blame others, myself, the world, and circumstances for my life.

Self-Blame Victim

I made bad or stupid choices. My life is my fault. There is something wrong with me. I am powerless to influence my life, world, and future.

External-Blame Victim

Someone, something external to me, has done me wrong. If this had not happened, then my life would be better. They did it to me, and there is nothing I can do about it. I am powerless to influence my life, world, and future.

Victimization: A frame of reference, experience, or belief (real or imagined, internal or external) involving blame that removes or distances power, choice, and action. Consciously or unconsciously accepting and believing that you are a Victim.

The last step on the ladder before achieving Personal Accountability involves some ambivalence. People try to hang on to the comfortable and familiar advantages of being a Victim while experimenting with the freedom of accountability. They start out by acknowledging that they can't always control events and that they have choices—a step towards consciousness and empowerment. But then they blame themselves or someone else for what is not working, keeping themselves stuck and powerless.

Think of the ongoing saga between parents and teenagers, the oft quoted lament, "You never let me do *anything!*" It's only a small exaggeration, but it speaks to the teen experience of desperately wanting power, yet being or at least believing they are powerless.

The Self-Righteous level of victimization is my favorite for several reasons:

- People operating at this level are usually close to a breakthrough.
- People at this level are often very entertaining.
- People at this level are, for the most part, really trying.

In general, self-righteous people have participated in some form of personal development process. They've done some consciousness work and understand, at least intellectually, that being a Victim is a powerless position. They no longer want to see themselves as powerless or to have others see them this way.

⭕ Consciousness Clue

It is generally people in the Self-Righteous stage of victimization who have the greatest difficulty saying, "I have been victimized, I am victimized, and I will be victimized in the future."

The Self-Righteous Victim says, "I know that I cannot always control or influence the events in my life but I *always* have a choice about how I will feel about them and how I will respond. I can do this and *still* blame others, myself, the world, and circumstances for my life."

What this means is that self-righteous people get that Personal Accountability is a powerful position. They

56

have decided intellectually that they will be personally accountable, but at an emotional level they are not yet able or willing to release the blame that they hold toward others or themselves. They are stuck in victimization, even though they talk a good game about accountability. They may even be doing their best to teach others about accountability in their homes, businesses, or classrooms. (I will be the first to admit that, before developing this work about Personal Accountability and understanding all of the subtle nuances, I spent time as a Self-Righteous Victim, even while telling others and believing myself that I was in fact being personally accountable.)

Here are some examples of what a Self-Righteous Victim can sound like.

I know my parents tried, and I am making the best choices I can, given my past and the fact that they were incompetent and should not have been parents.

I know that God is good, and I am developing a meaningful relationship with the universe, but the pain that my religion put me through in the name of God is unforgivable.

Notice there are three elements common to these examples. First, there is a clear, accountable statement. This is followed by "and" or "but." The third element that follows invariably has the hook of blame. In many cases, this hook is unconscious, the result of emotions making themselves heard in contradiction to the intellectual decision to be personally accountable.

⌕ Consciousness Clue

A wise man once said, "Everything that precedes the word 'but' is bullshit."

As entertaining and challenging as Self-Righteous Victims are, they still are closest to a meaningful break-through into true Personal Accountability. So, if you suspect you're still at this level, be patient. Commit yourself to learning in greater depth and detail how some of your blame and Victim energy still exists. Promise yourself that you are ready for the next step into the power of true accountability.

Tips for Identifying the Self-Righteous Victim:

- They are sure that they are *not* Victims.
- They often judge obvious Victims harshly.
- They can be eloquent about the virtues of responsibility and accountability.
- They tend toward Self-Blame rather than External-Blame.
- They are often disconnected from their emotions and hearts.
- Statements revealing their true emotional states frequently follow the words "but" or "and." When this is pointed out, they have elaborate justifications about how that was not what they meant.
- They have engaged in some sort of personal development or consciousness-training process.
- This section of the book focusing on the different types of victimization will be driving them nuts. They already know this, they say, and focusing on victimization is a waste of energy: "I've already done this, and I don't want to spend one more minute on it."
- They have demonstrable proof in their lives that they are now more powerful than they have ever been. At the same time, there are still some

recurring patterns of victimization that continue to bother them.

Accountable Language

As I was writing this segment of the book, I was eating in a restaurant in a small town in British Columbia. A young woman came in and began telling her friend, the waitress, and anyone else who would listen, about the trauma of her day. I can recite it word for word because I heard it four times before I left.

"You know my brand new eight-day-old car? Well, someone dented it! I was at work, stocking shelves, and as if that weren't bad enough, someone came into the store asking, 'Who owns the black car?' I asked if it was the *new* black car, and he said he didn't know. It was just a black car. So I went out to look and someone had backed into my brand new eight-day-old baby! To make matters worse, the dent is on the front right-hand fender, so, when people see it, they are going to think that I ran into someone. 'You know, women drivers!'"

Even though the event had happened only hours before, clearly the story was already well-rehearsed and much-repeated. Then the friend had to share her own experiences of having a new car dented, then a story about the flat tire they got last weekend, and when she said she had to leave, the first young woman asked, "What is he *making* you do now?"—yet another Victim story in the making.

This "ain't it awful" conversation lasted ten to twelve minutes, and there was not one accountable statement in the entire exchange. While it is true that the young woman was not directly responsible for the dent, she had clearly made choices that co-created the possibility. She had bought a new car, attaching extra significance to it as her "baby," and she chose when and where to park it. None of these choices created responsibility for the outcome, but they contributed to and set up the possibility of the event. Owning a car makes one eligible for a multitude of car-related experiences—hit and run, crashes, having your car keyed, and on and on. And all new and perfect cars must eventually no longer be new and perfect. I just want you to notice how much time, energy, focus and drama people put into retelling, reprojecting, and recreating their victimizations. In short, she is a perfect example of an External-Blame Victim, milking a common and easy-to-handle situation for all that it is worth. Do you recognize anyone you know in this example? Maybe even yourself?

The car owner spent a half hour in my hearing being a Victim, and probably twelve to twenty-four hours total over the next few weeks. What could she have done differently? Well, she might have driven to her body shop, gotten an estimate, decided whether to use her insurance to pay for it, and made an appointment to get it fixed. Total time: one-and-a-half hours.

How many times have you been stuck in a Victim story, milking it for all the attention and sympathy you could get, when in reality, in the big picture, it was nothing more than a slight inconvenience? I do not repeat this example because it is so unusual. I repeat it because it is so common. If you doubt this, go to any public space and listen to the conversations around you. Keep track of what you hear.

What percentage of the conversation are Victim based?

What percentage are neutral?

What percentage are personally accountable?

My Own Victim Dialogue

Before you do the next Activity, I will start you off with an example of internal and external dialogue after my own personal financial fiasco that I described in "My Own Victim Story" on page 40. As you'll see, I started with the External-Blame Victim position.

External-Blame Response: "I am hurt, wounded and stunned. This is difficult to comprehend. He was a rotten crook and a coward for killing himself. If that @#$% wasn't already dead, I'd kill him myself! Because of him, my plans for a company retreat in Mexico are gone. I am saddled with high-interest debt for years to come, like an anchor around my neck. I will have to work like mad to pay off this debt, and, because of this, I will miss out on some of the most important moments of my son's life. If this man had not stolen my money, I would be living my dream right now on the beach in Mexico. But he stole my money and destroyed my dream."

Time frame: This External-Blame response continued for two to three weeks, then diminished as the investors formed a committee to track down the stolen money and redistribute it to the partners. I moved from victimization to Emotional-Response Accountability. However, I confess I would have brief revisits to External-Blame victimization about every ninety days when the mortgage payment on the borrowed money was due.

Self-Blame Victim Response: "I was stupid, wrong, and incompetent. I let myself down, along with all my family and friends, because

I let them invest their money in my name.
How could I have missed the simple facts?
Why didn't I do more due diligence? How
could I be so irresponsible? I should know
better! People come to me for financial advice and support, and here I am, in debt and
working my ass off to make up for my incompetence."

Time Frame: This went on for a much longer
time than the External-Blame victimization,
probably three to six months, regularly triggered when my increased quarterly mortgage
payments were due.

Self-Righteous Victim Response: "Well, I
made the best choices possible. I managed my
risk, based on the partnership agreement by
pulling out profits. I was not alone. Many very
smart people—including the partnership's ac-
countant, tax lawyer, and securities lawyer—
were also involved. I tested the partnership
for almost two years before putting in my big
money. Cory and I interviewed the trader and
his wife. I did everything right!" (But then I'd
slip back into Self-Blame: "If only I had called
the phone number on the monthly statements
of the trading accounts, I would have discovered the fraud. I would have saved myself and
hundreds of others from this crook." And
from time to time I'd indulge in External-
Blame. Cory and I would be driving or watching TV, and one of us would suddenly say,
"That @#$%." Nothing else needed to be said,
and we'd just look at each other knowingly.)

Time Frame: For the next five to nine
months, my belief system reminded me, off

and on, that I failed to do the one simple thing I could have done. Or it would point out that if the trader hadn't been such a crooked bastard, none of this would be happening. Of course, these reminders would circle me back to Self-Blame and External-Blame victimization.

Activity – *Your* Victim Dialogue

Review your most significant Victim story and write a paragraph about your experience at all the levels that apply to you and your situation. What was your internal and external dialogue? What was the time frame of that experience? Is your victimization still going on? Be honest. Be sure to include your time frame. How long did you or have you been hanging out here?

Your Victim Dialogue

Your Victim Dialogue – continued

The Victim Pendulum

When I began researching this book, I noticed a common progression in how people move from victimization into accountability. There were three Victim levels, and nearly everyone progressed through them in a process that can best be described as a pendulum.

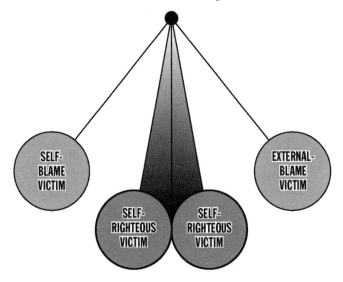

It generally starts with having some sort of External-Blame victimization. This may even be an inborn response to life. The small child blames inanimate objects for bumping into him—he kicks back at the toy that tripped him and rages at the floor for coming up and hitting him when he falls.

Then, somewhere along the line, our consciousness expands to acknowledging blame for ourselves. We begin to see that we play a part in what happens to us, and we expand on this to believe that everything is our fault. This may still be on the level of a child who feels guilty for every negative event from spilled milk to his parents' divorce. Or it could be more sophisticated

Self-Blame awareness, developed through the teachings of parents and society.

Over time and with increased awareness, we are exposed to a more sophisticated and complex view of the universe. We begin to see that victimization is not necessarily entirely our own fault or someone else's, so we find ourselves at the Self-Righteous Victim level.

The Self-Righteous Victim area on the pendulum chart is represented by the grey area about fifteen degrees either side of the center line that signifies no blame. When we are in this space, we believe that we "should" be accountable and we use accountable words, perhaps even talking about the lessons that we are dealing with. However, we are still blaming ourselves and others, although usually in a more subtle and sophisticated manner than in either the Self-Blame or External-Blame modes.

Most of the world actually believes that Self-Blame is being accountable or, in more common terms, responsible. In reality, for many it turns out to be just one more way to beat themselves up and diminish themselves. Consider this. One definition of the word "responsible" is able to respond or answer to something. Another more common definition is being the cause of something, often something wrong or disapproved of.

Are you more or less able to respond when you are busy blaming and beating yourself up? Is it possible for you to say, "Yes, I made a mistake," "I am responsible," or "It was my fault" and then *not* blame yourself? I believe you can, although it requires accepting what is. That's not always easy.

The reality for most of us is that our whole society is based on the concept of "responsibility," which is maintained by constantly establishing liability and blame when the mechanism doesn't work perfectly. Without practice and conscious effort, we rarely know how to release or let go of blame and move into Personal Accountability.

Of course, we could blame our parents and childhood experiences for this. Or, if we have moved on to accountability, acknowledge and understand that our filters were established at an early age.

Teaching People to Be Victims

Writing this segment of the book, I am sitting in a used bookstore and coffee bar (two of my favorite things in the world). The bookstore shares an entryway with a women's clothing store. I am positioned about twenty feet from the entry with a view into the clothing store, and both doors are propped open, letting a cool breeze pass through.

The woman who owns the store has brought her very cute sixteen-month-old girl to work with her. The little girl, by all standards, is very well-behaved. Right now, she is playing by herself under one of the racks of clothes, chatting up a storm, while one customer wanders and another talks with her mom.

The mother's behavior indicates that some unforeseen event required her to bring her child to work. Four times since I've been sitting here, the child has approached her mother, arms outstretched for attention, while Mom was dealing with a customer. And each time, the mother has turned her away by saying, "I don't want you," "I'm going to throw you in the garbage," and "I'm going to throw you in the toilet." As awful as this sounds, if I challenged her, I'm sure she would claim that she was just teasing. ("Can't you take a joke" is a frequent response from people accused of being rude or cruel.)

But think of such messages from the perspective of a small child, just learning language, just making sure that she is safe and loved. How else could a child interpret "I don't want you" other than, "There is something wrong with me"? If that becomes the filter through which this little one sees herself in the world, we have another Self-Blame Victim in training. If it isn't already obvious, the mom in this example is an External-Blame Victim, frustrated that she has had to bring her daughter to work. She may be angry at a child-care provider who has let her down or been delayed by circumstances. Whatever person, circumstance, or decision resulted in a difficult situation, the mother is taking it out on her child. Another example of how hurt people hurt people.

○ Consciousness Clue

As an adult, it is essential to understand your own Victim patterns in dealing with others who are impressionable, especially children. Children nearly always believe what you tell them. If you try to control their behavior by telling them that they are bad, they will believe it and prove you right. Your job as a parent (or mentor or teacher) is to do your best to instill positive messages that those in your charge are whole, complete, wanted, loved, amazing human beings with innate gifts as well as challenges— and you are there to assist them.

As I type this, the little girl in the dress shop has just accidentally or deliberately pulled on the phone cord, knocking the phone off the counter. She's gotten a spanking, and been told, "You are *bad!*" three times. Wait, there is more. Mom is now telling her daughter, "Gran'ma is coming, and she will spank your bum, too!" Gran'ma arrives, and the first words out of Mom's mouth are, "I spanked her bum because she is bad." Yikes! I can hardly stand it!

As much as I do not like to acknowledge it, this treatment of children is commonplace—God forbid, even "normal"—for many people. Is it any wonder that we live in a society where victimization is also "normal"?

Extending the Pain of Self-Blame

A coaching client of mine participated in a fundraiser for breast cancer. It was a 60K walk over two days. Her goal was to have fun, to raise $2,000 or more, and to walk the entire 60 kilometers.

On the first day of the walk, she experienced challenges, including not hydrating, getting sunburned, and feeling awful physically. The 30K that day took twice as long as it had in her training walks, ten hours instead of five. Day two was even more challenging, and she fell farther behind. Ultimately, to be present for the final ceremonies, she had to go the last two kilometers by car.

Results: she surpassed her goal of $2,000, raising $3,000 for breast cancer research. A wonderful achievement. However, she didn't have any fun. And for the next week, she beat herself up over not "doing it right." Her Self-Blame was amazing.

I failed because I didn't walk the entire 60K.

I failed because I didn't have fun.

I made dumb choices by not hydrating enough and letting myself get sunburned.

Her self-punishment was painful to everyone around her. I cannot imagine how agonizing it was to be on the receiving end of those harsh thoughts.

⌕ Consciousness Clue

Blame and guilt are closely-related negative emotions. If you feel guilty in your life, that is another clue that you may be operating in Self-Blame Victim mode.

When we are victimized, either by ourselves or others, and the victimization does not end with the painful event, there's a good reason.

The physical and emotional pain the fundraiser experienced on the second day of the walk was far less than the pain of the self-punishment that she continued to generate afterward. It may be obvious in this example that the ongoing self-beating was about more than the triggering event.

Continuing to blame and punish themselves after an event reinforces the negative beliefs of Self-Blame Victims. "See? I was right!" Limiting or negative beliefs are reinforced, providing a painful but soothingly familiar payoff. It is a cycle that perpetuates itself and can continue indefinitely.

Activity – Where Are *You* At?

All three levels of Victims can exist in one person at the same time, sometimes in different life areas and sometimes in the same area.

Most people are more comfortable with one of these three levels and use it more than the others. Identifying this level shows us where to focus our energy when we want to transition into Personal Accountability.

Right now, which of the three levels of Victims do you think you use most?

Which is most comfortable?

The Four Types of Victimization

Understanding the three basic *levels* of victimization, we can now look at the four *types* of victimization:

- Internal
- External
- Real
- Imagined

Internal: The ways we victimize ourselves such as negative self-talk, dishonesty with self, substance abuse, overeating, and, in extreme forms, addiction or self-abuse like mutilation.

External: What outside forces do to us, such as an educational, political, or cultural system

71

failing to meet an individual's special needs, or mental or physical abuse from others.

Real: Something that actually happened that can be objectively corroborated or proven.

Imagined: A perceived event that we believe occurred and that we choose to interpret as a victimization. For example, interpreting an expression of support and love as a negative comment about your incompetence; interpreting someone's confidence in your competence as a failure to rescue you and therefore proof that the person doesn't care about you; interpreting a friendly greeting as a come-on or threat; interpreting a negative response based on logic or logistics as a personal attack. (Imagined victimization can be difficult to identify and deal with because the Victim truly believes the victimization occurred, although it is a re-imagined and re-projected experience from the past.)

The Difference Between Internal and External

It's fairly easy to distinguish between internal and external victimization:

- Internal victimization happens in your inner landscape, internal dialogue, imagination, and feelings.

- External victimization is influenced or affected by something outside yourself.

The Difference Between Real and Imagined

How can we imagine being a Victim? A case can be made that if we believe a victimization has occurred, then it has. Our belief makes it real to us. However, truth requires facts rather than fancies. How can you decide if your victimizations exist only in your own interpretations or imagination, fulfilling self-created patterns and agendas?

Let's say you spot an attractive person across the room. You'd like to get to know this person, so you begin playing a mental scenario in which you go over to say hello—and end up being rejected. This rejection is so real and painful that you never actually go to speak to the person. You decide to skip the discomfort and have another drink or cream puff instead. Forever after, if you run into this person or even someone like them, you re-experience the pain of that fantasy rejection, adding it to all your other rejections, real or imagined. The imagination is a tremendously powerful tool!

Consciousness Clue

The human mind cannot tell the difference between something that has actually happened and something that is imagined with vivid emotion. The neurons fire in exactly the same way. So be careful what you imagine!

Let's explore the different combinations of these four types and see how they relate to our own patterns of victimization.

Real Internal Victimization

Unlike other kinds of victimization, most internal victimization is very real. Suppose you say to yourself:

- "I am stupid."
- "I hate myself."
- "I don't deserve to be loved, happy, or proud."

This internal victimization is just as real as if someone else shouted it at you. In fact, its negative effects are even more powerful than if someone hired a skywriter to write "Chris is stupid!" over the Super Bowl. You believe these messages because they are coming from the source itself (you), not some stranger. You can't dismiss it. You can't rationalize it by saying that someone else is just having a bad day and is taking it out on you. You *know* you're having a bad day and you know the reason why. It's because you are stupid, you are hated, and you don't deserve to be happy.

What is so fascinating about our negative self-talk is that often it is nothing more that a continuation of the external victimization that we experienced at the hands of our parents, teachers, siblings, and peers. The same self-diminishing thoughts that were generated by external victimization now get repeated internally.

How much of your negative self-talk is simply a repeat or an echo of what you heard about yourself and decided must be true years ago?

Imagined Internal Victimization

A classic example of imagined internal victimization is projecting something that has *not yet happened* and *imagining* what the pain, difficulty or challenge *will be*. Quite a feat of mental gymnastics. Yet, it is amazing how many people can achieve it.

They imagine taking a risk and failing: for example, starting a business that fizzles. And although they may never take the chance, their images of it are so vivid that they are able to experience the embarrassment and disappointment of this fantasy failure. Incredibly, this imaginary process will usually be followed up with real internal victimization, such as, "I am not smart enough" and "I could never deal with the financial consequences if I failed like that." Then along comes imagined external victimization: "My spouse might leave me" or "My family would ridicule or reject me." And this entire downward spiral has been triggered by something that *never actually happened.*

These spectacular psychological leaps would be fun to watch if they didn't have such sad consequences. Such negative Victim thoughts invariably limit possibilities, drain energy, reinforce powerlessness and, over time, actually manifest into objective reality.

Real External Victimization

This is the easiest to understand and identify. Someone did something to me, and I have suffered as a result. Being attacked, robbed, cheated, or abused are easy examples. Being harassed, lied about, or ridiculed can also qualify, as long as these are *real* events and cause you harm.

Imagined External Victimization

This type of victimization involves re-projecting a past victimization and imagining that a new situation is the same or similar when it actually isn't.

Here's an example that I observed firsthand. A young woman and her husband had struggled through some tough years but were finally able to buy the farm they had dreamed about. The woman's mother phoned and said how thrilled she was for them, taking this big step. The mother offered to visit and help with the cleaning, gardening, organizing or whatever was needed as they were getting started. I was present in the mother's home, and it sounded to me like a genuine offer of love and support.

A few days later, the daughter told me she had received a very upsetting call from her mother who had accused her of being incompetent "as usual" and incapable of running a farm.

When I realized that she was describing the same conversation that I had overheard, I was momentarily stunned. As so often happens in life, the daughter's reality was very different from my reality and possibly from her mother's reality. According to her perspective and interpretation, the mother's offer of help was a criticism. Was there an element of condescension, control, and intrusiveness in the mother's offer? Or was the daughter projecting the past, real or imagined, on the present and again seeing herself as a Victim? Obviously, these two women had a history with a lot of unresolved issues.

Consciousness Clue

Once we begin to notice and understand how we reproject our past victimizations onto the present, we can put our hearts and minds to work answering the question, "Which of my Victim experiences really happened, and which did I simply imagine and reproject?"

Activity – Your Levels of Victimization

Review each of the types of victimization and write one personal example of each.

Real Internal Victimization

Imagined Internal Victimization

Real External Victimization

Imagined External Victimization

Victim Games

In this section, we are going to investigate some of the different ways that victimization shows up in life—the patterns, the triggers, and the effects.

The Drama Triangle

This will be a very brief view of a behavior model called The Drama Triangle, created by Stephen B. Karpman, M.D. The three points of the triangle represent three key players. The first is the Victim, and if a drama has a Victim, there must be a Persecutor. Staying consistent with good drama and classic fairy tales, there must also be a Rescuer. (Shine up the armor and get on your white horse.)

Based on the labels at each corner of the triangle, which character do you most easily identify with? The reality is this. If we agree to play one of the roles, we actually play all of them. Let's look at the basic way in which the drama unfolds.

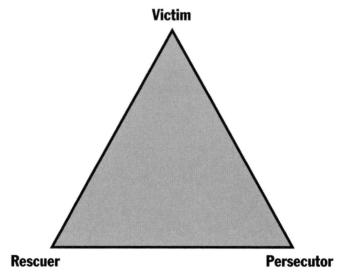

Victim

Rescuer   **Persecutor**

We start with our dear friend the Victim, who is in the midst of some persecution or other at the hands of the Persecutor. The Victim then communicates this horrendous situation in such a way—Victims have a broad repertoire of methods—that it attracts the attention of a Rescuer. The Rescuer does what rescuers do best. He or she swoops in with a solution, takes care of the issue, and all is well for now. The Persecutor is foiled for the moment.

On the surface, this looks pretty simple and even harmless. The Victim gets the experience of, "Someone cares about me. Someone loves me. Someone will save me." The Rescuer gets the experience of, "Aren't I amazing? Look at what I did. I am obviously significant and important because people need me."

Now, let's look a level deeper. Each and every time Rescuers ride in to save the day, they *do* send the message, "I care enough about you to do this." The insidious subtext, however, is, "Dear Victim, you are an incapable and incompetent boob. You cannot take care of yourself or your life, so I will do it for you."

In addition, Rescuers often find themselves too busy helping, fixing, and running around to create a life of meaning for themselves. They become more of a "human doing" than a human being. They define themselves entirely in terms of what they do for others instead of who they are.

Over time, Rescuers become weary of the unending task of saving Victims. The Rescuers then see themselves as Victims, with the former Victims as their Persecutors. The original Victims are now perceived as persecuting the original Rescuers, preventing them from living their lives. At this point, the original Rescuers-now-Victims do the unthinkable. They stop rescuing! The original Victims now have brand new Persecutors, the former Rescuers!

For example, a woman—who, by her own description has been and still is a Victim—saw herself and the end of her marriage in the triangle. Here is how the story played out for her. At the beginning of her relationship with her soon-to-be husband, she was attracted to his desire to protect her and keep her safe. This appealed to her greatly, so much so that in the early stages of the relationship she invented a telephone stalker, a heavy breather who scared her. This allowed her boyfriend to protect her by inviting her to spend nights at his place.

This type of deception and manipulation continued in their relationship, allowing her to get her needs met. When one crisis was resolved, she felt compelled to come up with a new one so she could continue to engage her husband. It went on for years, until he grew weary. Then a very real issue presented itself. She developed heart disease and required open-heart surgery. On the way to the hospital, she was talking to her husband about her fears and concerns. Instead of the usual sympathy, his response was, "Suck it up, princess."

The line was drawn. Her husband was no longer willing to be Rescuer, and she had a brand new Persecutor. After healing from surgery, she found she needed a new Rescuer. To fill this need, she had an extramarital affair. Thus, she assumed the role of Persecutor of her husband, the former Rescuer. The relationship disintegrated.

(NOTE: If it is not already clear, Victims caught up in the Drama Triangle always have some sort of drama going on. If you are involved with someone in this pattern, you will have experienced times when you solve their problem—being the great rescuer you are—and, within minutes, a new issue arises. Some people just can't get their needs met without a drama, real or imagined.)

Activity – The Drama Triangle

Think of a situation in your life when you have played one or more roles in the Drama Triangle. Describe the specific example. If possible, describe how, over time, you played more than one role. (NOTE: Sometimes it is necessary to cite several examples to see yourself playing all three roles.)

Games Victims Play

The Dutch sociologist Johan Huizinga described humans as *homo ludens*, the animal that plays. His highly regarded analysis, published in the 1930s, became fundamental to the modern study of cultural history. Huizinga theorized that every human activity—culture, society, politics, religion, love, and war—is a carefully devised game that we play by unwritten but generally accepted rules.

Taking this concept further in the 1950s, the Canadian psychiatrist Eric Berne developed a model for analyzing interactions, or "transactions," between individuals that he (not surprisingly) called Transactional Analysis or TA. His book *Games People Play* has sold more than five million copies.

Victims depend on games. They come up with a number of specialized games to maintain or enhance their roles as Victims. Here are some examples along with the rules and payoffs that these diversions provide. Learning to recognize them can be both amusing and useful.

Decide for Me

One of the greatest ways for a Victim to set up people is to engage them in a game called "I'm confused" or "I'm not capable of making a decision." The logic is that, "As long I don't decide, then I cannot be blamed for the outcome." This is a great example of Playing-Not-to-Lose.

The payoff when Victims play this game is that they generally keep from being blamed for not-so-wonderful results. The price is that they also never get any credit or acknowledgment.

Family and friends of Victims who play this game should be careful. Just because Victims do not want the blame of a negative outcome, this doesn't stop them from quickly blaming the person who *did* make the decision if things don't turn out well.

Support Me, but Don't Expect Me to Change

This is an interesting game. The Victim makes you into a therapist of sorts, calls for your advice, and gets you to listen to their woes. You (playing Rescuer) take them on as a fixer-upper project. The Victim will not really resist your support and suggestions, but at the same time will not act upon them or do anything differently.

Leave Me Alone

Over time, some Victims may withdraw further and further into themselves and into their safe little homes. It makes perfect sense. If you feel powerless, hurt, and unsafe, it seems wise to limit your exposure to whatever can hurt you. Agoraphobia, here we come.

A Victim who copes this way will always have a great excuse to keep from connecting, going out with people, and developing deep relationships. This can show up in behaviors like being a workaholic, especially in jobs where contact with others is limited, or in an addiction to chat rooms where one can socialize without the risk of real emotional intimacy.

Agoraphobia would be an extreme symptom, of course, bordering on genuine mental illness. As a side note, I have had many graduates who have been diagnosed with all sorts of mental conditions such as clinical depression, bipolar disorder, anxiety, and panic disorders, including agoraphobia. Many of these people, through awareness, support, and training, have been able to transcend their diagnoses. I believe that some mental illnesses are misdiagnosed, and, as a result, many in our society miss out on being taught how to redirect their thoughts and consciousness.

I Don't Like to Complain, But...

There is only one way you can win this game. Before the Victim gets to their big "but," quickly inject, "Then don't." It rarely works, but it is fun nonetheless. All that is going on here is a Victim seeking the payoffs and protections of victimization, while appearing not to be a Victim.

Oscar Contender

Over time, the Victim notices that the same old Victim stories don't produce the results they once did. To get the same much-needed attention, sympathy, and support, the stories need to be juiced up. I know a woman who is as sweet as a Victim can be. In the middle of a casual conversation, she'll slip in a statement like, "Yesterday, I fell off my bike and nearly died." She got a scratched knee and a bruised hand, and at no time was she in any danger of toppling over a cliff or being crushed by a speeding truck. However, in *her* mind she was near death. These performances can be pretty entertaining if experienced and observed from a slight emotional distance.

If You Think *That's* Bad...

This is a variation on Oscar Contender. It also relies on great dramatization skills, but the Victim tries to engage you in competing to see who has had it worse. It's a game of "Can You Top This?" and you'll always lose. Those who revel in this game are among the most obvious (and obnoxious) of all Victims, utterly unsympathetic to any of your own woes. You can think of them as the walking wounded, eager to bleed all over you so you'll acknowledge how tough their lives are.

Mike Tyson—Or Is That Scrappy-Doo?

A natural stage of victimization is the point at which the Victim decides, "Enough is enough. I will not put up with this kind of treatment any more." The Victim often becomes aggressive and is more than willing to bite your ear off, tell you they realize you have been abusing them, and announce they're not going to take it anymore.

This can be an admirable step toward accountability, but a problem arises when they are actually responding to external imagined victimization and their aggression is misdirected at innocent parties.

A variation on this kind of redirected aggression, often useful to society, is played by people who have been unable to fight for themselves against some form of real or imagined victimization. They resolve their frustration by taking up the cause of others whom they perceive as more victimized or less powerful than themselves.

I'm Fully Justified

This is the easiest game to spot. Just listen for the word "I can't because." For example, I can't:

- because of my kids/parents/spouse/ friends/*people*.
- because I don't have the education/talent/ connections.
- because I don't have the money/time.
- because I'm too old/young/thin/fat/tall/short.
- because of what *you* did.
- because *they* are against me.
- because of what happened in the past.

Justifications can be more sophisticated with more elaborate stories, more proofs, veritable spreadsheets of factual supports, even research papers documenting the incontrovertibility of the Victim position. The bottom-line message is that there is no way out. They are stuck absolutely and forever.

It's Not My Fault!

Sometimes deflected blame and ownership is stated outright. Sometimes it's just how the conversation is directed. I caught myself doing this one time, and simultaneously my wife, Cory, called me on it. She and I were facilitating a couples' weekend, and we were preparing in the classroom before the event started. Cory went to get herself a coffee, and I asked her to refill my travel cup. When she returned with my coffee, she told me that she had not put the lid on tight because her hands were full. I began organizing the handouts, and I knocked the cup over, spilling coffee all over everything.

I was grumpy about the waste of time, work, handouts, and coffee, and as I was cleaning up the mess, I said in a snarky tone of voice, "If *you* had put the lid on tight, this wouldn't have happened." Cory, who does not miss much, replied with a chuckle, "Funny. I was just thinking that if you hadn't knocked the cup over, this wouldn't have happened." A great reality check. I chuckled as well and apologized, and on we went to have a great weekend together. *That* is the benefit of understanding victimization and our Victim patterns. We recognize them for what they are, deal with them honestly, and move on.

I Quit

Victims will quit on you. It is one of the ways that they get to use and experience power. Note that they have already quit many times mentally before they actually quit in reality. In most cases, once they *really* quit, they are through. Don't waste time and energy trying to get them to change their minds.

I'm Hooked

Drinking, drugs, gambling, porn, sex, the Internet—the list of acknowledged addictions is ever growing in our society and is a direct reflection of our society's degree of victimization. Consider that the very essence of being a Victim is not having the power to do what you say you want to do. To be addicted to some external substance, process, or experience is the obvious continuation of the inner experience. Many people also become addicted to their own emotions, or rather to the biochemical level that feelings of victimization provide.

Here is how it works. Our body is a biochemical, bioelectrical machine. Every feeling and emotion is the result of electrical impulses in the brain that send messages to the limbic system, which manufactures special chemical signals called neuropeptides. There is a neuropeptide for every emotion you experience. They are released into the blood stream and rush out to dock on cells in your body. When this happens, the cell changes, eliciting the feelings and emotions that we experience.

This process is exactly the same for neuropeptides that are artificially created by outside substances like heroin or cocaine. When a cell that has been perpetually bombarded with the same neuropeptide divides, the new cells develop additional docks for that particular peptide. The body craves and needs that particular neuropeptide. We become addicted and attract people, events, and situations to us that will fulfill the addiction. (For more information, I highly recommend the 2004 film *What the Bleep Do We Know!?* and its 2006 sequel, *What the Bleep!?: Down the Rabbit Hole.*)

⌕ Consciousness Clue

You are addicted to anything that you cannot change. If you cannot change your Victim state, then you must be addicted to it.

People Are Stupid

This is an interesting game in that it allows Victims to be powerless and, simultaneously, superior to those whom they see as victimizing them.

You may know someone who enjoys this game. He or she has gone from job to job. In each circumstance, the boss or business owner turns out to be an idiot who doesn't know what he is doing. The coworkers are also incompetent, back stabbing, you-know-whats, and the customers are dumb as sticks. The list goes on and on. (NOTE: In addition to the workplace, this game can be played with romantic relationships, friendships, schools, teachers, and employees.)

There must be a cover story for the ongoing job changes, and invariably it is that others are doing it wrong. It can't be me, so it must be them. This is clearly someone destructively stuck in External-Blame.

Activity – Victim Games

Review the Victim games described above and identify the ones you've participated in. Do you have a favorite? Write a sentence about how each of the games you've tried plays out specifically in your life.

Decide for Me

Support Me, but Don't Expect Me to Change

Leave Me Alone

I Don't Like to Complain, But...

Oscar Contender

If You Think That's Bad...

Mike Tyson—Or Is That Scrappy-Doo?

I'm Fully Justified

It's Not My Fault!

I Quit

I'm Hooked

People Are Stupid

The Payoffs and Protections of Victimization

I have been telling you throughout this book that victimization is not accidental. This is a simple concept, yet at the same time it seems paradoxical. Intellectually, we are quite sure that we don't want to be victimized. So why do we play the game?

Simply put, Victims obtain two invaluable things: a payoff and protection. We as human beings do *nothing* unless there is something in it for us. Even the most selfless acts imaginable provide a payoff for those performing them. They get to reinforce their beliefs and prove themselves right about themselves, the world, and their place in it.

The same is true for victimization. When we choose to frame ourselves as Victims—and this is usually unconsciously—we get a powerful payoff that more than makes up for the discomfort, and we are protected from consequences, both real and imagined.

Now, some people are going to say, "Hey, wait a minute. That's not true! There's no payoff. All I get is pain, disappointment, and hurt—things that I want to be protected *from*."

Victim Payoffs

Don't let the word "payoff" make you think that a pay-off is positive, fun, or wonderful. Payoffs can be quite negative.

Think of a child who desperately needs attention and recognition. *All* humans do. If these basic human needs aren't met, the child will either retreat into isolation and mental illness or figure out a way to be fulfilled through negative behavior. Misbehaving and getting punished is better than being ignored, better than being an invisible non-person.

The same is true for adults who feel they cannot ask for and receive acknowledgement in a healthy and direct way. Victim patterns are nothing more than a method of getting essential needs met in an indirect and, at times, unhealthy manner.

Common payoffs include:

- Excuses
- Recognition
- Deception

Excuses

The primary payoff for Victims is that they get an excuse not to risk and not to be personally accountable. What kind of excuses can ongoing Victim framing provide?

- An excuse not to be completely independent
- An excuse to work fourteen hours a day
- An excuse to be alone
- An excuse not to ask for support and love
- An excuse to give up and quit
- An excuse to maintain addictions
- An excuse to lie and deceive others

- An excuse to settle for how it is
- An excuse to stay small

This list could go on indefinitely.

Before you do the Activity below about excuses, let me get you started by offering my own example. The theft of the majority of my net worth and of significant amounts of money from my friends, family, and staff provided me with the following excuses:

- Not to meet my financial goals of being 100% debt free by a certain date.
- Not to pay promised dividends to investors in Personal Best Seminars for two years.
- To go back to working fourteen or more hours a day, something I had vowed not to do.
- Not to follow my dream of moving to Mexico where I'd live on the beach and work only to train facilitators and coaches.
- To wear myself down and not take any holidays.
- To beat myself up for being stupid and incompetent.
- To start using my credit cards again.
- To take on an outside part-time job on the Investors' Committee, trying to recover the money.
- To ignore and avoid one of my businesses that was performing only marginally.
- Not to reward myself, as planned, with a beautiful classic collector Ferrari.

I could continue, but I think that you get the point. Now, what excuses is your victimization giving *you?*

Activity – Excuses

Your turn. Start with your most significant Victim story and write down *all* the excuses you got or are getting from that experience. Then continue to examine *all* the excuses that your victimization in general has provided you.

Recognition

Every human has a powerful, inborn need to be acknowledged by other humans. Being a Victim can fulfill this need, providing attention, importance, sympathy, reassurance, and even approval. The word "recognition" could also be replaced with a powerful little word that starts with the letter "L"—Love. Or at least what the majority of our world thinks of as love, which is someone paying attention to them and fulfilling some of their needs.

Recognition can work exceptionally well in combination with excuses to reward Victims. For example, "My boss victimizes me, making me work long hours, but he doesn't appreciate all that I do. If I go home and tell my little Victim story, and I do it really well, I can usually gain attention (someone listening to my story), sympathy ('Poor you for having to put up with such an ass for a boss'), and appreciation ('We really appreciate how hard you are working to keep a roof over our heads and keep food on the table')."

Consciousness Clue

Love is wanting for someone what they want for themselves.

Deception

Despite the presumably hopeless/helpless aspects of victimization, a compelling payoff is power—the power to leverage, control, and manipulate others and to maintain an image. Deception of others, along with self-deception, can be key elements. Victims will often downplay their skills, intellect, power, and capacity so that their Victim story is consistent and rings true. The Victim game of dramatization is a good example of this deception of others. (An example is the woman who fabricated a phone stalker so her new boyfriend would protect and take care of her.)

I know a man who decided he was being victimized by his wife's requests that he help around the house. He felt her performance standards were too high, and so she was persecuting him—a good example of the Drama Triangle. His solution was to deliberately screw up everything she asked him to do. Think pink laundry, broken crystal, and bills misplaced and paid late, costing a penalty fee. He is completely capable of such simple tasks, but to perform them competently would result in having to share the load. (Teenagers are also adept at this technique when asked to do household chores.)

Victim Protections

Being a Victim offers three basic forms of protection:

- Reinforcement
- Avoidance
- Justification

Reinforcement

Reinforcement proves that, despite what anyone else tells them, the Victims' beliefs are correct. These beliefs usually include themes like:

- I am powerless and helpless.
- I am incompetent. I can't measure up.
- I should avoid relationships that might fail and cause me terrible pain.
- I am far safer if I never try. The world is too frightening and dangerous.

What does *your* list look like?

Before you do the Activity below about your beliefs, I'll provide an example from my own Victim story. When I retold the tale of my loss, I told it so it reinforced and supported the following beliefs, both conscious and unconscious, that I had previously held.

- I have to work hard to succeed.
- I am not financially capable and responsible.
- Financial success cannot be easy.
- I cannot trust my own judgment.
- There is honor in overcoming hardship.
- Managing a crisis now is more important than planning meaningful contributions for the future.
- No good deed goes unpunished; doing something nice for someone else has consequences.
- It is not okay for me to be a "liquid millionaire" —to have a million dollars in cash or near-cash assets.
- It is not okay to be retired or semi-retired at the age of thirty-seven.
- It is not okay to live a life of creative leisure.

Activity – Reinforcement

What beliefs were or are you reinforcing through your Victim story?

Avoidance

The excuses that Victims make allow them to avoid a lot of things they fear or find unpleasant. There is also the basic human delusion that "If I pretend long enough that something isn't so, maybe it will just go away." (Yeah, that one *always* works!)

Justification

Proving you are right is a powerful form of protection, reinforcing and defending a favorite belief. What are you getting to be right about? What beliefs, conscious or less than conscious, are you reinforcing?

Every payoff and protection fills a need and offers a specific remedy. However, there are alternative ways to get your needs met in a more direct and healthy way. We will deal with these remedies in Part 3. For these remedies to work, you have to be clear and honest about what your real payoffs are and what beliefs you are reinforcing.

Letting Go and Moving Forward

The importance of analyzing and understanding payoffs and protections is that, once we know what is really going on (what needs are being met), we can let go of limiting beliefs and consciously try to get our needs met directly and honestly. Then we can move forward in our lives. To summarize:

Payoffs and Protections for Being a Victim
Excuses
For feeling superior, self-righteous
For not trying, not risking
For non-accountability, failure

Recognition
Attention, importance, sympathy, appreciation, approval, reassurance

Deception
Control, manipulation, leverage, maintaining image

Reinforcement
Maintaining beliefs

Avoidance
Of unpleasantness and things we fear

Justification
Proving you are right

Activity – My Payoffs and Protections

Answer each of these questions about your most significant Victim experience. Be honest. Otherwise the remedies won't work.

How has this Victim experience provided me with recognition—some form of attention, importance, sympathy, appreciation, approval, or reassurance?

How has this Victim experience provided me with an excuse—an excuse to be superior or righteous, to slack off, to fail or not risk, or not be accountable?

How has this Victim experience provided me with the need or ability to deceive others?

How have my deceptions served me by allowing me to control, manipulate, leverage, or maintain my image?

Which of my beliefs does this Victim experience reinforce, maintain, or justify?

What does this Victim experience let me be *right* about,
either consciously or less than consciously?

The Real Cost of Being a Victim

Before we end this segment, we must examine the
price that you pay long term in your life when you
choose to get your needs met through the Victim frame
of reference. We've looked at the payoffs provided by
the various games. Now let's look at the real cost of
playing Victim games.

We start by developing and consistently reinforcing the view that we are not powerful

enough to influence our life and world in such a way that we can be happy.
Real cost: We are unhappy and frustrated.

Then we attract and create relationships that reinforce this view. They generally start out just fine but soon degenerate into the same old cycle. These Victim games no longer work to get our needs met. The Rescuer becomes the Persecutor, and the Victim needs a new Rescuer. Relationships end with more drama and mess.
Real cost: We are unhappy, lonely, and in turmoil.

We view the world as unsafe, out of our control, and something to be cautious of and worried about.
Real cost: We are unhappy and frightened.

We don't really get to live our lives. We are doomed to repeat the same negative patterns over and over, thinking the same way, feeling the same way, learning little or nothing from our experiences. As Victims, we may survive, but we do not thrive.
Real cost: We are unhappy, frustrated, lonely, in turmoil, and frightened.

The long-term consequences of the Victim views of self and the world are that, the harder we struggle to get our needs met, the more we fail. All our experiences seem to prove that it is impossible. (Uplifting, isn't it?)

Once we're convinced that we cannot get our needs fulfilled, we look for others who can do it for us. This commits us to endless cycles of the Drama Triangle, alternately creating Persecutors and Rescuers who, because of the rules of the game, must always let us down, no matter how sincere they are and how hard they try.

Emotionally, Victim framing leads us to negative thoughts. As we become more and more trapped, the ratio of negative to positive thoughts gets higher and higher, and we become depressed. In *Authentic Happiness*, Martin Seligman, Ph.D. reports that depressed people have a 1:1 thought ratio, meaning one negative thought for every positive thought. People who are not depressed have a ratio of 2:1 or higher; that is, at least two positive thoughts to every negative one. We know that Victim framing attracts more victimization, bringing more negative thoughts. Is it any wonder that we have a depression epidemic in North America?

Physically, each of us has experienced feeling drained, weak, and sick when we are unhappy. Abundant research has shown that our immune systems are compromised by stress and depression. Recently, there has been an explosion of autoimmune disorders such as Hashimoto's and Graves' disease, fibromyalgia, rheumatoid arthritis, AIDS and many more.

Of course, the opposite is true as well. The happier, more grounded, and at peace we are, the stronger the immune system and the healthier the individual.

(If you are interested in exploring this further, some recommended reading is *You Can Heal Your Life* by Louise Hay and *The Secret Life of Water* by Masaru Emoto. A brief summary of Emoto's book is this. He put water in containers on which he randomly wrote positive and negative words. Some additional containers were blessed by a Zen Buddhist monk. Emoto froze the water and then photographed the ice crystals that formed. What is astounding is that water blessed by the monk created ice crystals of the most beautiful symmetrical shape. This was also true of the water from containers with words like "love" and "gratitude" taped to them. However, the containers with words like "hate," "kill," and "fear" all produced misshapen ice formations, some not even identifiable as crystals. Emoto's interpretation is that the positive or negative energy of words and thoughts physically affected the water. Now, think about that, considering our bodies are 80 percent water.)

Viewing ourselves and the world from a Victim's perspective is very hard work. It takes effort to carry and throw blame around. Imagine hauling a 100-pound weight with you everywhere you go. There are times when you get to leave it with someone else for a short while, but invariably you must pick it up again so it will be handy the next time you need to blame someone for something.

This weight also has another magical yet dubious property. It is so powerful that it can destroy anything positive, wonderful, and loving that it comes in contact with. The weight of blame can always find something wrong with any situation or circumstance.

So you're dragging around an enormous extra weight and it's robbing you of beauty, love, and wonder. Soon you need help. You need someone to help carry the weight, or at least someone to listen to how hard it is to carry. You become a Drainer, sucking support and energy from anyone, any time you can. You begin to seek out people and situations that can provide energy, and you begin playing Drainer games—relatives of Victim games. A case could be made that they are one and the same.

Action Steps

By now, it must be clear to you that shifting from Victim to being personally accountable won't be easy. It involves some loss of perceived security and recognition, and it requires significant risks as you abandon your excuses and Drama stories and put your ass on the line.

Reclaiming Personal Accountability requires designing specific action steps. Sometimes it is necessary to seek the input of others to ensure that these steps are appropriate and productive. Designing a program of action steps from a Victim's frame of reference can be disastrous.

For example, a woman in one of my courses had, in her own words, set up her life to be dominated by her husband, her boss, and other relationships. She enrolled because her efforts to end this perceived victimization had made her situation even worse. She had decided she wanted to "own her power" and "become personally accountable." However, her only frame of reference was either to dominate or be dominated. No middle ground, no co-equals. So, in an attempt to own her power, she went home to her husband and attempted to dominate *him*. After twenty-two years of being the boss (a role he may have assumed early in the marriage by default), he was unwilling to be dominated. Hardly a surprise.

She felt utterly defeated, powerless, and again victimized. Standing up for herself obviously didn't work. Why? Because she had created her action steps from a Victim's frame of reference: "I am not going to let them victimize me anymore. (Therefore, consciously or unconsciously, I am going to victimize *them*.)"

This *never* works. What she needed was coaching and support to help her see how power is shared in a relationship. When she got it, she was able to create conscious agreements about power and redefine her relationships.

Victims who take their Victim framing into the design of their action steps can actually reinforce their Victim experiences. Outside support is generally needed.

Consciousness Clue

> If you catch yourself in Victim mode and want to break the cycle, be careful that the actions you choose won't result in more victimization. Engage a coach, a friend, or an accountable neutral third party to help you design your action steps and to support you in framing the outcome. (For professional assistance with this, please see Appendix 3 at the end of this book.)

Your reward will be energy, improved relationships, honesty, expanded consciousness, and much more. This brings us to our final activity on Victims, weaving together specific action steps to help you make the transition.

Activity – Letting Go

Please complete the following sentences.

To let go of my victimization, I am willing to:

More specifically I will:

Tell the truth about what you really want in life. Write the truth as you perceive it today here.

Let us say that you decide to engage in a process to become more conscious of your beliefs, releasing those that block and limit you and strengthening those that support and inspire you.

(If you don't know what this could look like, I strongly suggest that you review the Appendices at the end of this book for special offers from Personal Best Seminars. You will find online programs, one-on-one coaching, and, of course, with the purchase of this book you get the five-day seminar "Personal Best Level One, The Truth Revealed" *free.*)

Write what your process will be.

Again, let us say that you decide to fulfill your needs and get your payoffs in a more direct and healthful way. Write specifically how you are going to do this. (NOTE: if you are not yet clear about this, Part 3 will assist. For now, give it your best shot.)

Finally, let us say that you have decided to take clear and conscious risks, and lots of them. What are the specific risks that you must take to let go of your victimization?

What You've Learned So Far

Well, I, for one, have had enough of examining the nuances of victimization. I trust that:

- You have a clear picture of what being a Victim is.

- You are willing to accept and be honest about responding to victimization in your life without using it as a frame for becoming a Victim.

- You can identity your overall level of victimization.

- You can distinguish between real and imagined, internal and external victimization.

- You are aware of your primary Victim games and can recognize them in others.

- You truly get that, within your victimization, there are real needs being met in indirect and expensive ways through your payoffs and protections.

If you cannot apply each and every one of these statements to your life and your victimizations, please go back and review. Understanding and acceptance is essential to making the transition to Personal Accountability.

Consciousness Clue

What if there is no one to blame? Not even yourself?

PART 3

The Personal Accountability Experience

Being personally accountable is an incredibly freeing and joyous experience. It focuses you on creativity, solutions, meaning, and evolution. However, the first step toward accountability is something that is outside the experience or framework of the average person. That's why it can be so difficult for so many.

The first step is to ask yourself: What if there is really no one to blame, not even myself? If you are like most people, right now your brain is doing some version of, "Don't be so stupid. There is always someone to blame and if there isn't, I'll *find* someone." Yes, I know. We can always find someone—all those rotten someones out there (or the rotten someone within).

Personal Accountability takes the position that blaming yourself or anyone else is a big waste of time and energy, not worth the payoffs and protections.

Let's revisit the pendulum that seems to be the natural process of learning to be personally accountable. Most of us swing back and forth between two extremes, External-Blame and Self-Blame. Over time, many of us settle a few degrees left or right of the center line, living the life of a Self-Righteous Victim. Then the pendulum stops moving and hits dead center. It is from that position that we are able to climb through the three levels of Personal Accountability—from Emotional-

Response Accountability to Practical Accountability and, ultimately, to Spiritual Accountability.

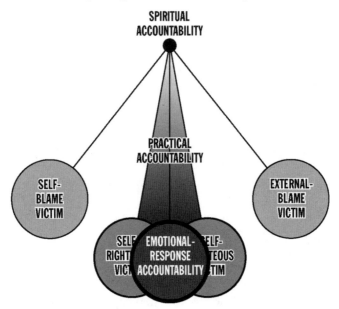

Once we arrive at the grounded position of the center, we can use a tool called "experience and observation without judgment." From this neutral position, we can see reality much more accurately, use our precious energy much more wisely, and learn in a more complete and engaged way.

I recognize that giving up blame is a lot to ask, that it really doesn't fit within most people's view of the world. That's exactly the reason to give it a try. I am going to ask you to set blame aside. You can pick it up again at any time if you choose, but for right now, choose to believe that your time, energy, and life are too precious to waste on blaming yourself or someone else. Try the following affirmation, saying the sentence aloud three times:

"I choose to release blame."

If you have trouble, try closing your eyes and remembering a specific victimization situation. Then symbolically forgive yourself or the other person. For example, imagine a cloud of blame evaporating from the other person's shoulders or visualize yourself setting down a great weight of blame. Tell yourself:

> My life and energy are too precious to be consumed by blame of self and others. I choose to release blame, and I direct my energy back to what I control and have significant influence over.

The Three Levels of Personal Accountability

Now let's start by reviewing the definition and levels of Personal Accountability:

Personal Accountability: A framing device that eliminates blame of self and others, providing the power of choice, participation, and co-creation of the experiences and results in our lives, real or imagined.

Spiritual Accountability

I am a Spiritual Being having a human experience. My purpose here is to experience myself, remember who I am, and evolve at a spiritual level. I co-create everything based on this. I even choose my parents, and I choose the time, place, and method of my death through every choice I make in my entire life.

Practical Accountability

I co-create my results and experiences in life. I focus on my choices without blame. There is a lesson in everything, and I choose to find it.

Emotional-Response Accountability

I cannot always control or influence the events in my life, but I always have a choice about how I will feel about them. I respond without blame.

NO BLAME

GENERATOR

Emotional-Response Accountability

This is the most basic level of accountability and the beginning of personal power. Reread the definition:

> **Emotional-Response Accountability:** I cannot always control or influence the events in my life, but I *always* have a choice about how I will feel about them. I choose to respond *without blame.*

When you master this, something magical and amazing happens. Events can no longer dictate and control how you feel. You *always* have the power and capacity to choose how you feel and how you are going to respond.

With Emotional-Response Accountability, you choose to direct your energy to the only three things in the universe that you can control: your thoughts, feelings, and actions.

Consciousness Clue

The difference between reacting and responding is the difference between being a Victim and being personally accountable.

The premise of Emotional-Response Accountability is that there is *only one person on the planet* who has the power to choose your emotions. Guess who that is.

This level of accountability is exceptionally valuable for dealing with issues, trauma, and drama when they are happening. It helps us to step away from the painful experience and observe without judgment, consciously choosing our emotional state, and doing whatever is necessary to deal with the situation at hand.

116

⌕ Consciousness Clue

No one has the power to make you feel anything—hurt, hate, love, or joy—unless you give
them that power.

This is a concept that many people have trouble
with. How can we *not* feel profound pain when terrible
things happen to those we love, or experience joy
when marvelous things happen? But think of it this
way. While you've been reading this, hundreds of children have starved to death, thousands of people have
died in accidents and wars, and cruel injustices have
taken a terrible toll on humanity. Most of us have made
a conscious choice not to let our emotional concern
incapacitate us and keep us from responding intellectually and practically. We choose not to give power to
these events. Of course, personal tragedies and loss require grieving. It's normal. But then some get stuck in
the process and continue to surrender their power to
outside forces. With Emotional-Response Accountability, you take back your power as soon as possible.

A Burning Question

I want to give you a practical example of Emotional-
Response Accountability. My friend Glenn was going
through some difficult times. First, his family business,
a lumberyard started by his dad more than twenty-five
years earlier, went bankrupt, causing many difficulties
for him personally and in the family.

But Glenn, being a resilient person and an entre-
preneur, saw that all was not necessarily lost. He realized
that one branch of the business, a truss manufacturing
plant, was always profitable. In fact, it had been carrying

the lumber operation for some years. (Trusses are the angled wood structures that support the roof of your house.) So he made a proposal to buy back that portion of the business from the bank. They sold it to him, and he started over. The deal was challenging and difficult, but he was soon exceeding his profit projections. He had the business on a steady footing, and his dad was back working with him. I was proud of his tenacity and hard work, and so was everyone who knew him.

You're sensing that this is not the happy ending of the story, and you're right. On his way to work one morning, Glenn's cell phone rang. It was his foreman calling to tell him that the shop was on fire, and the fire department was on the way. By the time Glenn got there, the blaze was out of control. The fire department was not as interested in putting out the fire as in keeping it from spreading to nearby businesses. Glenn said it was the most helpless feeling he'd ever had, watching everything that he and his family had worked a lifetime for going up in smoke.

By 9:00 A.M., the entire business was ash and rubble. Glenn, his dad, and the shop foreman retired to a nearby coffee shop to discuss what to do. Throwing in the towel was a very real choice and, frankly, what many would have chosen to do in his place. However, the response he chose was to stay true to his business, his plans, and his purpose.

Before noon that day, he had rented a truck bay as a temporary location and arranged to use some of his competitors' excess capacity to keep his agreements with his customers. Then, he began contacting customers to let them know what had happened. His business, his building, and all his manufacturing capabilities were gone, but he would still be delivering their trusses.

Please do not miss the key distinguishing factor that makes this story an example of Emotional-Response Accountability and *not* of Self-Righteous victimization. From the moment the three men sat down to discuss how to cope with this crisis, they didn't spend one second of time or one ounce of energy discussing who or what was to blame. If they had, you can be damn sure that Glenn would not have been able to reopen the business two hours later. The tragedy had happened. Nothing could change it. The fire inspectors and insurance company could sort out the details later. Right then, there were agreements to keep and a business to rebuild.

Glenn still runs his truss company. Today, it is one of the largest in Calgary, approximately 4,000 percent larger than the day it burned to the ground. That is the power of Emotional-Response Accountability.

When You're Abused

I am often asked, "How can *I* be accountable for being abused as a child?" When this question is in the frame of Emotional-Response Accountability, it generally means that the asker is still confusing the word "blame" with "accountability."

If you were an abused child (or if you were criminally victimized by someone else at any stage in your life) you have no responsibility for the event itself. However, you can be personally accountable for the following:

- What you decide about yourself after the experience.
- How the experience impacts your relationships and your life today.
- What beliefs you form about other people.
- How often that experience from the past gets replayed in your head.

When you achieve Emotional-Response Accountability, you realize that the issue is not about what has happened. It is about how *you* choose to respond.

Someone tried to gain power over you by subjecting you to a negative and destructive event. You regain power through your response. This is much easier to do if you are clear about your purpose and mission in life. Each provides you with a rudder to steer your life and your actions, not only in times of difficulty, but day by day and moment by moment. I am a big fan of Stephen Covey's work. His discussion of mission statements in *The 7 Habits of Highly Effective People* offers one of the best approaches I have come across. I still use the mission statement I first created more than fifteen years ago, using a format from his book.

My Own Emotional-Response Story

Before you do the next Activity on choices offered by Emotional-Response Accountability, I'll provide you with a brief example of how I used internal and external dialogue to deal with my financial loss. My self-conversation went something like this.

"Well, if this has really happened, what are my choices? How can I deal with this in the best and most proactive way possible for me, my friends and family, and everyone else hurt by this?"

Later, I was able to recount the proactive steps that I took. First, I participated in forming an investors' committee to find and reclaim any assets left by the trader and any of his companies. I had found out about his death on a Sunday, and two days later I helped to coordinate a meeting of the larger investors. We hired counsel and a bankruptcy trustee, and, two days after that, we got a judge to sign a petition to move the companies into bankruptcy. We acted quickly and efficiently.

We did our best to set blame aside, so it would not hinder our efforts or blind us to what was really happening.

Time frame: My choice started as soon as the shock and disbelief wore off, about a day or two after the trader's death, and it continues to the present. My choice assisted me in dealing with the pain and consequences of the event as it was happening.

Activity – Your Emotional Responses

Your turn. What could be (or is) your experience and dialogue, internal and external, from the perspective of Emotional-Response Accountability? Review your most significant Victim story, and this time write a paragraph about how you *could* choose to feel about it and respond to it. (NOTE: Some of you may have already done this in your life. If so, take this opportunity to write down specifically how you chose to respond. Remember, the key is to do so *without blame*.)

Practical Accountability

This level of Personal Accountability builds upon Emotional-Response Accountability, but adds two very significant elements:

> **The concept of co-creation** assumes that human beings are always creating—creating thoughts, creating feelings, creating relationships, creating money, creating cells, creating structures. To use the dreaded double negative, you can't not create. You are a creation machine. Therefore, we as humans have participated in or co-created (at some level) every result and experience of our lives.

> **The concept of finding a lesson** imagines that we can learn from our experiences. (What an earth-shattering concept!) Sarcasm aside, this concept isn't new, yet so few people apply the lessons of their experience. If you question this, consider the persistent patterns in your own life. They are recurring because you have been unable or unwilling to interpret them and apply the lessons.

All results and experiences have the three kinds of input that we have talked about before (inputs we control, inputs we have various degrees of influence over, and those inputs that simply affect us). Co-creation acknowledges that there are results and experiences in life that you *can* control and others that you do *not* control. When you are conscious of the part you play in controlling these experiences, you are then able to frame meaningful lessons from the results you obtain.

122

Co-creating

In their book, *The Power of Personal Accountability*, Mark Samuel and Sophie Chiche describe three levels of participation when you co-create events:

Creator: Your behavior is the direct cause of the situation.

Promoter: You are not directly causing the situation, but you are enabling or encouraging someone else to cause it.

Allower: You are participating by *not* participating. You are allowing the situation to continue by silently standing by and doing nothing to prevent it from happening.

Let's use an example of a common victimization, lung cancer. While scientists have found some other causes, the vast majority of cases can be traced directly to smoking or inhaling second-hand smoke. Knowing this, here are some examples of co-creating in the three levels of participation:

Creator: I smoke, or I choose to work or live with smokers.

Promoter: I buy cigarettes for my partner, spouse, friends, or children.

Allower: I let people smoke in my house or on my property, in my car, or in areas near me that I control.

Co-creation is both a strength and a challenge. The strength is that it assists us to analyze each situation and result, separating the thoughts, choices, and actions that contributed to any experience or result. For many, the challenge is to separate out what is ours and what is not. It's tempting to focus on the significance of other contributing factors. The minute we do, we begin our slide down the slippery slope of blame.

◯ Consciousness Clue

You consciously co-create your experiences and results when you focus on *your* choices without blame. There is a lesson in everything when you choose to find it.

My Co-creating Story

About twelve years ago, my wife, Cory, and I were driving home from my office late one night. We were stopped at a red light, when, out of the blue, *thwack!* We were rear-ended by an obviously intoxicated driver and hurled forward into the intersection. No one was hurt, just shaken up. Our car was badly damaged, but drivable.

Now, in this situation, there were clearly many inputs that we could not control or influence. However, we chose to focus our energy on what we *could* control, the part of the situation that we had co-created:

- We *choose* to drive an automobile, and we do so being clear and conscious of all potential risks including personal injury and death.

- We had *chosen* to be on the road at a time when statistics say the number of drivers who are under the influence of alcohol is very high. (It was a summer weekend, just after last call in the bars.)

That's it. Those were the obvious choices we had made to co-create an accident happening at that time and place.

Now, there is one other part that we may or may not have influenced. We, of course choose to believe that we did influence it. Cory and I had been talking for a couple of months about getting the car painted. It was a great, reliable car that we liked, but the paint was fading and it was looking a little rough. One of our considerations was that, at the time, we were a one-car household. How would we do without a car for the time it would take to get the car painted?

One of the outcomes of this car crash was that the insurance company provided a rental car for a month while our car was shipped to a friend's body shop out in rural Saskatchewan. The car was repaired and completely painted, and it now looked like a million bucks, all for the price of just the repair if we'd had it done in the city.

I believe that this outcome was a direct result of being accountable, not getting caught up in blame about what that rotten drunk did, how he could have hurt us seriously or even killed us, the inconvenience of insurance claims, etc. We could have focused on how, if it weren't for the clients who had made me work late and the route we'd chosen to drive home and the people who'd sold the liquor and the drunk insisting on driving his car and the hassle of the insurance adjustors, we would not have had any of this inconvenience, blah, blah, blah—or more accurately, blame, blame, blame. You get the point. We skipped all that and went straight to a solution.

Activity – Participation in Co-creation

Co-creation can yield both negative and *positive* results. First, write three examples of how you have co-created *positive* results or experiences in your life for each of the ways to co-create:

Creator: The situation I created was

The way I did this was

Promoter: The situation I promoted was

The way I did this was

Allower: The situation I allowed was

The way I did this was

Now, describe three examples of how you have co-created *negative* results or experiences in your life for each of the ways to co-create:

Creator: The situation I created was

The way I did this was

Promoter: The situation I promoted was

The way I did this was

Allower: The situation I allowed was

The way I did this was

Finding a Lesson and Applying It!

At the level of Practical Accountability, the lessons we can learn are generally about the practicalities of living in the world and coping with life, love, and relationships. What we are really talking about is discovering and consciously attaching meaning. Victor Frankl, author *of Man's Search for Meaning* and many other books, created *Logotherapy* which literally means "therapy through meaning." Sigmund Freud said humans have a "will to pleasure" and Alfred Adler described "the will to power." Frankl theorizes that we have a "will to meaning." I believe this is true and forms a fundamental pillar of Personal Accountability.

Business Lessons

An early experience in my business relationships was that I would enter into verbal agreements with partners, employees, and others. Then later on we'd find that there had been a misunderstanding or misperception that would cause stress and strain, and could even end the relationship. The lesson I learned, while not rocket science, was to put all business agreements in writing. So simple, yet it eliminated the vast majority of misunderstandings. I did not dwell on whose fault the misunderstanding was or whether someone was deliberately trying to victimize me.

Primary Relationship Lessons

How many people do you know who have been married twice, three, or even four times? One could assume that these love-challenged individuals have some difficulty learning the lessons that present themselves in their relationships.

When I originally attended the Personal Best Course (the predecessor of The Personal Freedom Program), I had just experienced the end of a primary relationship with the woman I loved (yet I was so afraid of intimacy that I couldn't tell *her* that). As a result of the lesson I learned, I committed myself to honesty in relationships and even created an agreement with myself to go back and have a heart to heart talk with the woman I loved so that we could leave the relationship in a clean, clear way, get on with our lives, and have a better chance in our next relationships.

That conversation, in which I clearly expressed my true feelings, had a monumental impact on my life. The woman I loved, Cory, became my wife.

Financial Lessons

Again I will provide you with a personal example using my financial loss experience. When I let go of placing blame, I was able to ask:

What were my choices that co-created this event?

- I chose to take the word of the person who recommended the investment, instead of doing my own due diligence.

- I chose to leverage my most significant assets, my commercial building and home, by putting a high-interest, high-ratio second mortgage on them and investing the proceeds in the fund.

- I chose, after two years of the fund performing well, to let my friends, family, and employees invest money in my name in the fund (because I thought I had secured the last spot in the partnership).

- I chose to pay less attention to my core business, to become semi-retired for a year or so, relying on the income from my investments.

- I chose to maintain a high-leverage position to maximize the amount of money working for me in the fund by not paying off my credit cards, thus increasing my debt.

What were the choices I made to deal with the event after it occurred?

- I chose to participate on the Investors' Committee, to do my best to reclaim and redistribute money to partners in the most fair and appropriate fashion.

- I chose to learn how to trade myself and hired two trading coaches.

- I chose to create a recovery strategy for me and my business.

- I chose to hire a personal development coach to assist me in maintaining focus and consciously creating a meaningful lesson.

- I chose to dig myself out of the hole and search for the lesson that this could provide.

What is the lesson I choose to attach to this event?

- I must become both responsible and accountable for my financial success. (This was the second time in my life when I had invested significantly in another person, wanting them to "do it for me.")

- I must educate myself, make my financial freedom a priority, and build upon my innate skills to do so.

- I must stop looking externally for my financial success. It is not somewhere over there. It is right here if I choose to apply myself.

What are my action steps?

- Focus on making a greater contribution to my community and the world. For example, during our fifteenth anniversary. I chose to give away 1,500 Personal Best Level One "truth revealed" courses, a value of $1.5 million. We have also dedicated ourselves to supporting the United Nations Millennium Project goal of ending poverty in our generation. (Visit our website at www.personalbestseminars.com for more information about how this book, Personal Best, and our friends and associates are making a difference in an African village.)

- Focus on my skills and unique experiences by writing a book and creating related materials, all focused on how to be personally accountable.

- Eliminate *all* debt with the exception of mortgages.

- Create "super reserves" of cash, equity, and credit.

What was my time frame?

- I was working at this level of accountability around two to six weeks after the event.

- My choices were almost immediate, but the lesson and the application of the lesson took more time.

Spiritual Accountability

Some dismiss the idea that our purpose here on earth is to learn and evolve. If we are spiritual beings, they contend, then we already know and are everything, so we are here only to experience ourselves. In my own view, even to experience ourselves as something we have not experienced before implies learning a lesson and applying it. By doing so, we may co-create an even better world.

Another common belief is that learning is best achieved through pain and tribulation. If that has been your experience with learning, I ask you to reconsider. Learning can exist in both pain and joy. Right now in my life I am on an exceptionally steep learning curve, being a new parent. These lessons have been beautiful, joyful, amazing, and meaningful. How can I describe my love for a child, a love that existed even before he physically came into our arms and our lives? Lessons need not be hard. They can be joyful, even fun.

Let us explore both of these elements in more detail. First, I want you to consider carefully the meaning of co-creation as it is expressed in the first part of the definition of Spiritual Accountability. Read the initial three sentences aloud slowly:

> I am a Spiritual Being having a human experience. My purpose here is to experience myself, remember who I am, and evolve at a spiritual level. I co-create *everything* based on this.

"That's a pretty broad statement!" you may be saying. "How could it possibly be that we create *everything* in our lives?"

Personal Accountability: A framing device that eliminates blame of self and others, providing the power of choice, participation, and co-creation of the experiences and results in our lives, real or imagined.

NO BLAME

GENERATOR

Spiritual Accountability

I am a Spiritual Being having a human experience. My purpose here is to experience myself, remember who I am, and evolve at a spiritual level. I co-create everything based on this. I even choose my parents, and I choose the time, place, and method of my death through every choice I make in my entire life.

Practical Accountability

I co-create my results and experiences in life. I focus on my choices without blame. There is a lesson in everything, and I choose to find it.

Emotional-Response Accountability

I cannot always control or influence the events in my life, but I always have a choice about how I will feel about them. I respond without blame.

Sometimes in my seminars, I pose questions about such spiritual beliefs. Suppose we are, in fact, timeless and divine spiritual beings, currently engaged in a human experience. Would it then be possible that we are fulfilling a contract that was made before we existed in this physical form? I don't care whether or not the seminar audience or you believe in these possibilities. What I want is for us to consider them—to see if a spiritual belief at this level resonates. You may reject the entire concept as nonsense and choose to concentrate on Practical Accountability. That's okay. Or you may choose to believe in Spiritual Accountability as well, not because it is "right" or can be proven, but because believing that you have choice, power, and co-creation in your life empowers you.

The last sentence of the Spiritual Accountability definition focuses very clearly on just how huge the degree of that empowerment can be:

> I chose my parents, and I choose the time, place, and method of my death through every choice I make in my entire life.

If you're sitting there, shaking your head and muttering, "Now you've lost me!" let me explain.

No Accidents and No Miracles

First of all, choosing our parents seems biologically impossible. We can't choose the humans who produce us or the humans who raise us. We're stuck with the genes we're born with, along with the place and time we come into this world. But with Spiritual Accountability, we are not talking about biology; we are talking about soul, spirit, divine essence.

The idea of choosing our deaths seems equally shocking. Yes, people *can* control their deaths by choosing suicide or selflessly sacrificing themselves to save someone in danger. We all know stories of people on their deathbeds who wait for an event or the arrival of a loved one before they pass away. At the level of Practical Accountability we merely *influence* the time, place, and method of our deaths by the millions of choices we make throughout our lives—choices like diet, health habits, high risk behaviors, profession, those we associate with, and where we live. Those who live where tornados, floods, hurricanes, earthquakes, or volcanic eruptions occur are taking a calculated risk, but then natural disasters are characteristic of nearly every area of our planet. Those who choose to drive cars, fly, ride on buses or trains, swim, play football, or jog are aware on some level that these activities can be dangerous. Even those who never leave home are also in jeopardy statistically.

But again, with Spiritual Accountability, we are talking about more than just the mechanics of choice in a physical form. We are also talking about soul, spirit, divine essence, and the interplay between our divine and human selves.

Of course, it's possible to have no *obvious* control or influence over your death. The thousands who died in Hiroshima or the World Trade Center certainly didn't, beyond living in a violent world. Someone struck by a falling meteorite may have practiced stellar personal habits and yet fail to survive. But the position of Spiritual Accountability is that even the most unlikely "accident" has meaning at a spiritual level—meaning that we, at this physical level, do not and cannot precisely understand. However, that doesn't have to stop us from searching, asking, and attaching meaning that we believe could be linked to our spiritual evolution.

If we are spiritual beings, it is possible that we co-create all kinds of experiences with others to fulfill contracts or agreements that have meaning for our souls or divine selves. From the human perspective—a perspective deeply rooted in the dichotomies of good/bad or right/wrong—some of these experiences seem meaningless, cruel, and "wrong." We may begin to ask questions like: Does God (the universe or whatever you want to call it) make mistakes? Is there divine order on the planet? Is there really more to me than flesh, blood and bones?

But we could also ask a different kind of question. For example, what if the citizens of the more than eighty nations who died in the World Trade Center had a spiritual contract to participate in reminding the United States—the most powerful nation on the planet—of its co-creative capacity not to wage war and confront terrorism, but to bring an end to poverty and suffering worldwide? What if the tragic events of 9/11 reminded the superpowers of their supreme ability to contribute?

What if the money spent on war could go instead to participating in economic development? Not the kind of "aid" that so often passes as a cover for manipulation and aggression, toppling leaders uncooperative with the superpowers. Instead, a real empowerment of individuals in the poorer countries so they could escape victimization and take charge of their choices and destinies. What about sending fax machines and cell phones instead of weapons, so people could communicate with each other, and maybe foot-powered water pumps and solar generators for areas without electricity? What about grassroots family-to-family sharing, like the millions of C.A.R.E. packages that were sent to Europe following the devastation of World War II? In personalized acts of giving, individuals sent packages of necessities one-on-one to victims of the war—even in formerly "enemy" countries—speeding the healing and rebuilding process.

The key point of asking questions of this different kind is that if we get to choose what we believe the spiritual evolutionary implications of events are or might be, we may as well choose something significant. Why choose blame and retribution—the beliefs of victimization—when you can choose beliefs that lead you out of victimization to a higher level of Personal Accountability?

> We are not permitted to choose the frame of our destiny. But what we put into it is ours.
> *Dag Hammarskjold*

Think about that for a moment. There is meaning and purpose in everything. Whether you choose to believe something is good or bad, right or wrong, it has meaning and purpose at a higher level. Spiritual Accountability—the highest level of accountability—takes the position that there are no accidents and there are no miracles. There are only contracts and co-creation.

Now read the full statement aloud again:

I am a Spiritual Being having a human experience. My purpose here is to experience myself, remember who I am, and evolve at a spiritual level. I co-create *everything* based on this. I chose my parents, and I choose the time, place, and method of my death through every choice I make in my entire life.

Stop for a moment and check in, physically, mentally, emotionally, and spiritually. How does it feel? Intuitively, does it feel true? Does it feel false? Does it feel scary and uncomfortable?

Let's be clear. I do not know for certain and I cannot prove to you that this statement is true, yet I feel that it is true, and, perhaps more important, I *choose* to believe this statement because it encourages me to be personally accountable.

Please understand that this is an idea that is outside the belief systems of many people. Yet, it is hardly a new idea. It has been around virtually since the first human being asked the question, "Why am I here?"

In her book *Sacred Contracts*, Caroline Myss describes Mithras, the Greek/Persian god of contracts, who was supposed to help humans set up agreements with the gods before coming to earth. On this journey, the humans would bathe in the river of forgetfulness to erase their memories of these pacts, yet their divine contracts would remain in effect. So, the idea of sacred contracts about our purpose on earth is an ancient one.

Consider this possibility. What if, before you assumed your current physical form, you made an agreement or a series of agreements with other spiritual beings or with the universe itself? And then you took this physical form to experience what you had agreed to experience?

Consciousness Clue

If there is divine purpose in *everything*, then there are no accidents and there are no miracles.

Does This Mean Our Lives Are Predestined?

I do not believe that we are predestined, that our lives are laid out for us in advance. That would eliminate the power of choice, which is one of the most powerful concepts in the universe. What makes the most sense to me is that we make contracts on general themes— themes that I believe become our missions in life.

If, for example, my mission has a theme of forgiveness, what kinds of experiences might I have in living my mission? Would I experience being a person who needs to forgive? Or would I be a person who needs to be forgiven? What if the theme of my mission is self acceptance? Would I have lots of experiences that build my self esteem? Or would I suffer many experiences that might rob me of my self esteem?

Accepting the concept of Spiritual Accountability provides a framework for attaching meaning to the unknowable: consciously or less than consciously, we choose to draw people and experiences to us that provide us with opportunities to live and fulfill our missions.

I believe that Spiritual Accountability is one of the most powerful ways to answer some of the difficult questions of Personal Accountability—questions like:

- How can I or others be personally accountable for my childhood abuse?
- How can I or others be accountable for the horrors of war, murder, starvation?

The *how* is the easy part. More to the heart of the matter is: Do you or others want to be personally accountable for abuse, war, starvation, or any other commonly viewed "awful or horrendous" event? Spiritual Accountability asks the question: What is on the other side of the coin? Nothing is created one-sided. Ask yourself: What could this experience contribute to my spiritual evolution?

Let's look at an all too common experience: sexual abuse. Sexual abuse wounds people deeply and can cause untold versions of limiting beliefs. It has long term manifestations such as sexual dysfunction, shutdown or promiscuity; fear of the gender of the abuser; depression; obsessions, and low self image. The list goes on and on.

But what if someone who experienced sexual abuse chooses to believe that this very negative experience is part of their mission in the following ways:

- To stop the cycle of abuse in their family.
- To have empathy for others and help them to heal.
- To learn and experience forgiveness.
- To recognize that we are spiritual beings as well as physical beings.

With each of these possibilities comes meaning, freedom, choice, learning, and contribution. Each of these provides the framework for conscious engagement in life and evolution at a human and spiritual level. This is the essence of Personal Accountability.

Spiritual Accountability starts when you can ask:

- What is the deeper spiritual meaning in this experience?
- What is the other side of this experience for me?

With the foundation of Emotional-Response and Practical Accountability solidly behind you, the answers to these questions are often clearer, simpler and easier to find.

> There is no such thing as chance, and what to us seems the merest of accidents springs from the deepest source of destiny.
>
> *Friedrich von Schiller*

Again I will provide you with a brief example from my own experience.

My Spiritual Accountability Experience

One of my recurring Victim thoughts after I lost all that money was, "If this hadn't happened, I would be on the beach in Mexico right now, building a retreat and training coaches and facilitators."

To achieve Spiritual Accountability, I needed to build on my position of Practical Accountability and consider the flip side. I had to ask myself, "What is the deeper spiritual meaning of this?"

I decided that the flip side of, "I would be on the beach" was:

> My work at Personal Best is not done yet. There is something very meaningful about what I have created here, and my most significant contribution is yet to come. I choose to believe that this event is one more

message I co-created with my higher self, the universe, and those around me about my mission on this planet. I believe this mission is to be personally accountable and to share my vision of Personal Accountability. This book and the body of work that will follow is the application of that deeper spiritual meaning for me.

Time Frame: My progression was very quick. I had created the chart and structure of the Evolution of Personal Accountability by the middle of January 2005, only about three weeks after finding out about the collapse of the trading company. I have been developing, refining, and sharing this information in various formats with thousands of people even before this book.

⌕ Consciousness Clue

We choose all our beliefs, consciously and less than consciously, to help us make sense of and cope with the world. Some of those beliefs may no longer support us. If all our beliefs are chosen in the first place, why not choose beliefs that support us in feeling happy, joyful, and purposeful?

Becoming a Generator

Once you begin to wrap your head and heart around dealing with the mechanics of life at the practical level of accountability and you explore the broader arching lessons of spiritual evolution, often a pattern begins to emerge. You discover that the lessons you are learning are related, not random. Cumulatively, they will answer your question, "What is my mission?" More on this in the final segment of the book.

Indicators That You Are a Generator

Of all the benefits of accountability, one of the easiest to observe is what life is like when you stop draining yourself and others and become a *generator*. Most people instinctually get what this means, but let's answer the question, "A generator of *what?*"

The short answer is, "a generator of whatever you focus on—energy, love, acceptance, money, support, wisdom, knowledge, connection—the list is almost endless."

When you're a generator, you experience synergy. Amazingly, the effects of the whole become greater than the sum of the parts. One plus one no longer equals two. Now, it equals eleven.

Here are some clues to recognize when you are being a generator:

- People seek you out and want to be with you.
- You can be alone and feel optimistic, powerful, and loved.
- You have the capacity to give without feeling less or drained.
- You have clear boundaries and create relationships where they are respected.
- You have personal integrity. You keep your word with self and others.
- Your self talk is encouraging, generally positive, and propels you forward

Indicators of Personal Accountability

How can you tell if you are actually being accountable? Be warned. Initially, there are times when we flip back and forth between victimization and accountability several times within the same thought. This is common. Even when you dedicate yourself to Personal Accountability, you still have all those old Victim stories, triggers, and patterns in your memory. Be patient. It takes time, practice and purpose.

To support you along the way, there are some milestones that you can look for to see if you are on track.

Early Indicators

- Using I-me-my centered language
- Being grounded in reality, honest with self and others
- Applying the remedies for your payoffs and protections
- Engaging in life solutions
- Framing conversations around applying lessons and learning

Long Term Indicators

- Consciously choosing beliefs
- Choosing resourceful and empowering emotional states
- Minimizing meeting needs through payoffs and protections
- Enjoying a high level of resiliency
- Experiencing relationships that work
- Changing results by applying lessons

PART 4

How to Become Personally Accountable

Now that you see the entire evolution of Personal Accountability and understand the levels, experiences, and results that each creates, let's focus on how to *be* personally accountable.

Your question is, "Exactly how do I respond to whatever event has just occurred without getting sucked into blame?" Remember how I said that I see accountability growth as a pendulum. It may be helpful to study the pendulum chart showing how we must center ourselves before we can rise through the stages of growth.

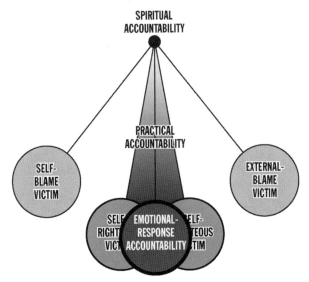

Let's start by acknowledging the process in general.

The External-Blame Victim: Most of us start by blaming others. Many have had External-Blame experiences that we have carried around and retold, reprojected, and recreated for years. We have told ourselves (and maybe others) that if this or that had not happened, our lives would be very different and so much better.

Then, at some stage of the game, we get tired of the story. We suddenly realize—by reading a book, taking a course, going to church, or having an epiphany—that our results weren't entirely caused by the rotten bastard who victimized us. In fact, we also have played a role (sometimes a very significant role) ourselves. We think, "Well, if it isn't all someone else's fault, then it must be all *my* fault." In that instant, the burden of blame shifts from the external he-she-it-they-them to ourselves.

The Self-Blame Victim is usually the next stage of the pendulum swing, internalizing all the blame that we have been aiming at others. (It is also possible to reverse this process, starting at Self-Blame and swinging over to External-Blame.)

Note that people in a Self-Blame mode often mistake their position for being personally accountable.

The Self-Righteous Victim is represented in the illustration by the grey area about fifteen degrees either side of dead center. When we are in this space, we believe we have become accountable. We use accountable words and even talk about the lessons we have learned. However, we are still hooked on blaming ourselves and others.

Emotional-Response Accountability is represented with the pendulum dead center, not a single degree to the left or right. In this position, no energy is wasted on blame of self or others. However, the slightest motion can easily swing the pendulum off dead center and into blame of self or others.

Practical Accountability takes the position that we co-create all the experiences and results in our lives, and that there is a lesson or meaning in everything that occurs, providing we are conscious enough to seek it out and apply it.

It is represented halfway up the vertical axis of the pendulum, midway between Emotional-Response Accountability at the bottom and Spiritual Accountability at the top. To reframe your Victim experiences and move toward Practical Accountability:

- Focus on the choices that co-created the Victim experience.
- Use accountable language: I–me–my.
- Don't waste any time or energy on blame.
- Use your emotions for action, not reaction.
- Identify the lesson and articulate how you can or are applying it to your life.

Note that from this pendulum position closer to the fulcrum, it is more difficult to swing over into blame. If you do, it is generally to a far lesser degree and for a shorter period of time.

Spiritual Accountability is the fulcrum, centered at the top of the pendulum. It is the position of absolute power from which the rest of the model moves. Here, you have the broadest perspective and can see how all the parts of the model are related and work together.

People who have reached this pinnacle can say and mean, "I am a Spiritual Being having a human experience. My purpose here is to experience myself, remember who I am, and evolve at a spiritual level. I co-create *everything*, based on this. I even choose my parents, and I choose the time, place, and method of my death through every choice I make in my entire life."

Shifting into Accountability

The purpose of this recap is to remind you that victimization is a natural process, but that you have choices about how you are going to deal with it. With that in mind, let's shift to being accountable.

Let Yourself Feel Victimized (for a Time)

I know this seems counterintuitive, but do not ignore the last part of the statement, *"for a time."* This is an important aspect of telling the truth and being authentic. It is a great test of your capacity to acknowledge and work *with* the natural laws of the universe.

How long is "for a time"? That depends. For me, it's as long as it takes to acknowledge my feelings, framing, and then making the conscious choice to be accountable. It doesn't have to be long. The longer you spend being a Victim, the less conscious you are of your options. The only thing that would be less productive, from my perspective, is denying that victimization occurs in my life in the first place.

In a universe where we control only three things (by now, you know what they are), there are millions of forces that influence and outright affect us. Victimization is normal and natural. Your only question should be, "How long do I choose to be a Victim?"

Do Your Own Personal Work

This seems so obvious, yet most in our society have not fully engaged themselves in consciousness work. This entire book is one framework for beginning or laying the foundation of becoming conscious.

For starters, here are some reminders.

- Personal Accountability is not right, and choosing to be a Victim is not wrong. They are both valid choices at different times for different reasons. No one can make you be personally accountable. It is an internal event that you *choose*, and, in that choice, you bring yourself closer to the experiences of power and co-creation in your life.

- The process of being accountable is generally preceded by spending some time as both an External-Blame and an internal Self-Blame Victim.

- The primary hallmarks of accountability are the absence of blame and the capacity to articulate and apply a lesson. The more significance you place on the lesson, the easier it is to be accountable.

⌕ **Consciousness Clue**

We create what we need to be in alignment with what we believe.

Activity – Self Awareness

Here are some self-awareness questions. (If any of these questions are tough or too difficult for you to answer, then you have work to do, because these questions hardly scratch the surface of leading a conscious life.)

What are your three most significant limiting beliefs?

1.

2.

3.

What are your three most supportive beliefs?

1.

2.

3.

What is the most significant payoff you get for your recurring negative patterns?

How do you take care of yourself?

Physically

Mentally

Emotionally

Spiritually

What is your motivation to take care of yourself in those ways?

Are you in debt? What does that say about you and your belief system?

Is your job or career in alignment with your life purpose?

What are your spiritual beliefs? Can you articulate them? Do you live your life in alignment with them?

What is your life mission?

Use Accountable Language

Many times throughout this book, I have suggested using I–me–my language to frame your beliefs and actions. This is one of the foundations of Personal Accountability.

Our society tends to say "you" and "we" when in fact we are talking about ourselves. If you question this, watch any television interview program. The interviewee says things like, "When *you* are in a situation like that, *you* just react automatically" or "Anytime *you* lose, *you* feel devastated." These people are clearly talking about themselves but substituting "you" for "I-me-my." They distance themselves from the experience, which reinforces and actually sets them up to be a Victim.

So, each and every time you talk about yourself, find a way to say it in the first person. Use *I*, *me*, and *my*. For example:

Unaccountable: "When you are in a situation like that, you just react automatically."

Accountable: "In that situation, I reacted automatically."

Unaccountable: "Anytime you lose, you feel devastated."

Accountable: "When I lost, I felt devastated."

This pronoun shift may seem like splitting hairs, another version of "you say *po-tay-to* and I say *po-tah-to*." However, it is much deeper and more significant than that. Every time the words *I*, *me* and *my* are used, your belief system goes on notice: This is significant. This is important. This is about *me*.

Accountable language develops authenticity, transparency, and personal power. It acknowledges the truth about most communications. Whenever we open our mouths, no matter what the topic, we are really talking about ourselves, our beliefs, and our perceptions.

When people start working with the concept of Personal Accountability, they often say, "I am taking accountability." My first reaction is always, "Where are you taking it from?" The reality is that early use of this phrase usually describes the shift from External-Blame to Self-Blame or from Self-Blame Victim to Self-Righteous Victim.

Identify Your Payoffs and Protections

This is a huge and complex topic that could fill an entire book by itself. If you've done the Activities related to this concept, you probably have a pretty good idea of what your past Victim payoffs and protections are. However, most people haven't the foggiest idea how to address their own needs or fulfill them in a healthier, more direct manner.

⌕ Consciousness Clue

You have needs, I have needs, Maslow's hierarchy has needs. (If you didn't think that was funny, Google "Abraham Maslow.") The clearer we are about natural and healthy human needs, the more directly we can get our needs fulfilled, the more consciously we can align our lives, the less energy we consume to fulfill our needs, and the more we can grow, enjoy, and evolve.

Payoffs and protections are indirect and largely unsuccessful attempts to get our needs met. Each of the following remedies is designed to be a direct approach to fulfilling our needs.

Recognition Payoff: Attention, importance, sympathy, appreciation, approval, reassurance.

Some people choose to be Victims because it is the only way they know to get recognition. Think of all the things that you have done in your life to gain recognition. Another word for recognition is love (or a reasonable facsimile thereof). You've made sacrifices for loved ones, sometimes just going along and pretending you agree, all to make sure you are not judged or rejected. Human beings do wild and wacky things to be recognized, to fit in, to be loved and accepted. The truth is, it rarely works in the way that we would like it to.

Recognition Payoff Remedy: It's so simple and yet nearly impossible for many people. Simply *ask directly for what you want.*

"I beg your pardon," you say. "If it were that easy, I would already be doing that. I remember times in my life when I asked directly and I did *not* get what I asked for." I understand that, and of course you're right—at least from your perspective. That's why you created the devious routines you have to get the love and recognition that you need.

Let's elaborate on the deep and complex idea of asking directly for what you want. Sometimes, we're afraid that if we describe what we truly want and ask for it, we are giving power to those who want to hurt or thwart us. However, consider the logic of *not asking*, but hoping that someone in your life will catch the hints, intuit your deepest desires (which they should, of course, if they truly care about you), and then behave as you desire. This is nothing more than preplanning and preparing to be victimized by the people from whom you want love and recognition.

Here are some guidelines for successfully asking.

- Ask directly and honestly for what you want.
- Ask someone who has the capacity to give you what you are asking for. Asking a starving man to give you food is unproductive. Asking someone incapable of a committed relationship to provide eternal fidelity and devotion is a recipe for disaster.
- Ask, knowing that it is the other person's *choice* to give to you or not. They have every right to say "no." That doesn't in any way dismiss or diminish your desire or need. Develop a support network broad enough that you have more than three people to ask.

But suppose you have co-created your relationships in such a way that asking for what you want directly would be nothing more than a setup for the other person to exert power over you by saying "no." Then start by renegotiating the ground rules of your relationships *before* asking. Some relationships descend into a spite war, an arena where each resents the other for not supplying what is needed, so they punish each other by withholding what the other wants. If this has happened, negotiate a truce and a new agreement about how you will interact with one another. Your objective: If either of us asks directly for what we want, and the other is physically, mentally, emotionally, and spiritually able to provide it, they will. If they can't, they will explain why and offer support for fulfilling this need in another way.

To summarize: If one of your payoffs is recognition (and it is if you are human), ask directly for what you want, ask someone who has the capacity to give it to you, and remember to ask with no strings attached.

They have every right to say "no," and you have every right to have your needs fulfilled.

Excuses Payoff: To avoid trying and risking, and to justify non-accountability and failure.

Excuses offer major protections to Victims. Think of all the little ways that excuses make your life easier. Besides justifying the major dramas and traumas, excuses are the day-to-day standby of Victims. So what are some typical examples?

- I would like to start my own business, but the economy is weak.

- I would like to start my own business, but I couldn't put in the hours it would require. My family needs me.

- I would like to start my own business, but my parents won't lend me the money.

- I would like to start my own business, but I'm not good at selling.

Such negative self-talk alternates between External-Blame and Self-Blame victimization. Even simple, everyday language, such as "I have to...," "I can't...," "They made me...," is all Victim framing and has even *more* impact and effect on your life than the big excuses provided by traumas and dramas.

Excuses Payoff Remedy: The best way to stop using Victim excuses is to become personally accountable.

I know this seems a bit simplistic, but it's true. We co-create victimization to provide ourselves with excuses, and we use the excuses to continue being Victims. Breaking the cycle by using accountability is the only remedy.

Ask yourself what the excuse is really for. Usually, there is a cover story with a real excuse underneath.

For example: "I would like to start my own business, but I can't because I'd have to move to another area which I can't afford and which would hurt my family." At first glance, this seems like a money and family issue. However, this may not be the case. It could actually be that the person feels incompetent and unskilled in business. It could be that the speaker once failed and is afraid to try again. Or it could be that he or she simply doesn't want to work that hard. It could be anything, but be clear that it is usually not the first-level excuse.

⌕ Consciousness Clue

Excuses like "I don't have enough time" or "I don't have enough money" are, for most people, first-level excuses. More honest would be, "I have the money, but my time is consumed with working for money." Or "I have the time, but I don't generate enough money to do what I want." The actual excuse should be, "I have not yet learned how to balance my income, expenses, and time to live the life I say I want."

Think of it this way. We love excuses that work. Once we find them, we keep using them. Two good ones with some social acceptability are "I don't have enough time" and "I don't have enough money." One way to find out what is really going on is to focus on what the excuse protects us from rather than the content of the excuse itself.

For example, I had an exceptionally talented person working for me who had the capacity to contribute, accomplish, and earn far more than he was. The excuse was, "I'm not ready yet." The truth was that he was so afraid of failing that he was unable to take the risks necessary to live his dream. He eventually realized and admitted this. In his case, "I'm not ready yet" was an excuse not to risk failure.

Deception Payoff: Control, manipulation, leverage, and maintaining your image.

Lying, prevaricating, fudging, double-dealing, telling little white lies, cheating, deceiving, social lies, and outright whoppers—in many cases, civilized society discourages the absolute truth in every situation if it is rude, crude, or will hurt someone unnecessarily. It's all too easy for dedicated Victims to adopt the custom and protect themselves by deceiving others.

Deception Payoff Remedy: You're going to be shocked. The remedy for ending Victim payoff deceptions is to tell the truth.

Imagine that. How deep and complex! Yet, telling the truth is difficult for most of us. When I say to tell the truth, I don't mean simply to say, "I lied. Here is the truth." That's the smallest aspect of the process.

What is most significant about this deception is your motive. What need were you or are you attempting to fill? Telling the truth means being authentic, transparent, what-you-see-is-what-you-get. Giving up the payoff of your victimization means you're willing to communicate your wants and needs honestly. In relationships, you're willing to create agreements about how you want to be treated and how you will treat others. You establish boundaries and enforce them. This means putting all your cards on the table. People can choose to like you, love you, judge you, or hate you. When you are being authentic, you know you are being accepted or rejected based on who you really are.

This is the only type of acceptance or love that your belief system will actually allow. If you're in a relationship where you pretend to be something that you are not, you won't trust any love and acceptance you receive. You know you were acting, so the acceptance must be for the act, not you. In this situation, you must dismiss the love, and you continue to feel unconnected, unaccepted, and unloved, even though you tried so hard.

Honesty is more than telling the truth. It includes communicating the fears, motivations, and hopes that you tried to manage through the deception.

(While honesty has always been "the best policy" and is essential for escaping victimization, it may be an even more productive habit, given new lie-detecting technology.)

Victim Protections: Reinforcement (maintaining current comforting beliefs), justification of actions (proving you are right), avoidance of unpleasant or difficult situations and things we fear.

A brief reminder: Every payoff offers a protection at the same time. This is how your belief system is wired. Your belief system will go out of its way to prove itself right, even if this causes you pain.

For example, if you have learned and accepted a belief that says, "People cannot be trusted," then, to prove your belief is correct, you will attract and co-create relationships, situations, and events that will *prove* that people cannot be trusted, even if those situations cause significant pain in your life.

⌕ Consciousness Clue

Your belief system will go out of its way to be right, even if it causes you personal pain.

CALVIN AND HOBBES *Bill Watterson*

CALVIN AND HOBBES ©1993 Watterson / Dist. by UNIVERSAL PRESS SYNDICATE
Reprinted with permission. All rights reserved.

Victim Protections Remedy: When you understand and accept that your beliefs are limiting you and causing you pain, your remedy is to consciously risk counterbalancing your limiting beliefs.

If the primary protections gained from being a Victim are reinforcing and justifying your limiting beliefs, then risking is the logical way to get yourself moving and leave your limiting beliefs behind.

Of course, any old risks, willy-nilly, won't do. They must be designed to counter the old limiting beliefs. Let's say that you believe that people cannot be trusted, and that belief is part of your excuse for not engaging in relationships, not putting out your business ideas, and not being completely authentic. Then, you need to design a risk that includes trusting, being authentic, and developing healing relationships.

For example, one of the limiting beliefs I developed when my parents got divorced was that primary relationships don't work. Now, I was not consciously aware that I held that belief. It was more like a pair of glasses that I did not realize I was wearing but which was obvious to anyone who saw me or talked to me. To me, it was not so much an opinion or belief as a simple statement of fact. I could have backed up this "fact" with all the latest divorce statistics, the number of people I knew from single-parent homes, and the number of people in unhappy relationships. You get the point.

It was not until I participated in The Personal Best Course (the predecessor to The Personal Freedom Program) as I told you in Part 3, that I became conscious of my belief about primary relationships and recognized that it didn't work. It was just a theory that I had gone out of my way to *prove* correct, so much so that while I was participating in the seminar I was heartbroken because the woman I loved had just broken up with me.

This was when I began to examine all the choices I had made in that relationship, trying to prove that primary relationships don't work. I was astounded. From the very beginning, I had put the wheels in motion for the relationship to end. I started the process "on guard," wanting to make sure that I would not be hurt when the inevitable end came. I did whatever I could to protect myself from having my heart broken. I withheld myself. I had no intention of actually falling in love with her. When I did, I was not honest about it, and, if we had trouble, I would point to the facts and statistics that relationships themselves just don't work. It was not my fault.

Then, I became conscious of my payoff excuses and my deception of others. I decided to remedy them and try something new. Here is what I did. I called my ex-girlfriend and asked to come and see her to talk. Please note that it was not my intention to get back together with her. I just wanted to end the relationship in a clean, clear, and honest manner so that both of us could get on with our lives and create relationships that work. She agreed to see me.

I made the three-hour trip, and all the way my stomach was in knots. I knew that I had to learn and to apply the lesson. I had to risk telling the truth about how I had participated in our relationship and the truth about how much I actually cared. I wanted to become personally accountable—to talk about my choices and my lessons—but it scared me to death.

To put into perspective how scared I was, I have walked on fire, jumped out of airplanes, gone hang-gliding, rolled cars, and fought with a burglar who was breaking into my home. None of these experiences brought me even remotely close to my level of fear of having that conversation. It was one of the most difficult things I have ever done and, in hindsight, one of the most valuable.

At the end of the conversation, we hugged each other and wished one another the best. I left feeling as though each of us could start fresh, confident that I would not carry the pattern forward and neither would she.

Then an interesting thing happened. Because of the honesty and authenticity we both exhibited that day, we remained friends. We continued to respect each other and participate in each other's lives. The end of this example is my favorite. That woman is now my wife. Cory and I have been together since 1984, and it would not be possible for us to have created our happy life together, a life we are so proud of, if I had not taken that risk to counter my limiting belief.

The Remedies Summarized

Recognition Payoff Remedy: Ask directly for what you want.

Excuses Payoff Remedy: Be personally accountable.

Deception Payoff Remedy: Tell the truth.

Victim Protections Remedy: Take conscious risks to counterbalance your old limiting beliefs.

Applying Remedies

If you have followed my examples, you will have noticed that taking any sort of action to remedy and change Victim payoffs and protections involves an inherent risk.

Asking directly for what you want involves a huge risk. If it didn't, you would already be doing it.

Being personally accountable is one of the biggest risks in the world. It jeopardizes the structures that have been limiting your capacity to participate in your life, making it a fraction of what you are capable of.

Telling the truth is another huge risk. What if there are consequences? What if people don't like you anymore? What if people see you for who you really are? What if they find out you are a fake? What if you are judged?

Taking action on any one of the remedies puts you in risky territory, but facing those risks and taking those steps will move you forward in your life significantly.

What if you're still unwilling or unable to risk? At least take the time to decide what you are protecting with your current behavior. What are the beliefs that you are maintaining or reinforcing through the Victim payoffs? Once you can clearly identify them, you prepare yourself to counter your old, outdated beliefs the next time they limit you.

Tell yourself the truth about your life and the situations that you have not been willing to face. Arnold Schwarzenegger, governor of California and three times Mr. Universe, said that lifting weights while visualizing the specific muscles he wanted to strengthen was a hundred times more effective than just lifting the weights. I believe that the same is true for applying the remedies for payoffs and protections. These remedies all involve risk, but consciously taking the risks to counter or disprove the old limiting beliefs can have a hundred times the impact of risking unconsciously and hoping all will work out.

Focusing on the Lessons

Why do people have so much difficulty recognizing the lessons their Victim experiences can teach them? I believe this is because the lessons are positioned directly in our blind spot, right under the victimization that has been the source of pain, frustration, and powerlessness. The Victim story is so big, bright, and obvious that it eclipses the lesson that is right behind it.

Think of it this way. The victimization and the lesson are the opposite sides of the same coin. Imagine that you are walking along a dirt path in the sun and a shiny object catches your eye. You go over to it, and, gleaming in the sun, is a bright, shiny quarter. When you pick it up, you notice that the back side is still covered with moist dirt that takes a bit of work to brush off. Finally, you can see that the other side is just as shiny. However, you would never have found the coin if it had been flipped over, shiny side down.

The same is true for your Victim story and its lesson. It is easy to see the Victim story because it is polished and shiny from being replayed in your head so many times. However, the hidden lesson on the other side needs a bit of work to reveal itself before you can tell yourself the truth about your life, your Victim experiences, and the lessons that you have not been willing or able to face.

What do I mean? Well, think of it this way. There has to be a reason why you haven't been able to learn and integrate the lessons from your recurring Victim experiences. That reason is the truth about yourself that you have not been willing or able to tell. Here are a couple of examples:

- A young woman who consistently chooses men who are not as powerful as she is was not able to break the cycle until she told the truth: that she would never give her heart completely to a man who was less powerful. By continuing her pattern, she could keep her heart safe (and her relationships unfulfilled).

- A young man who has tremendous capacity keeps himself small, does not completely commit to his dreams, and resents and holds negative energy towards those who do what he would like to. The truth he must tell himself is that he lacks the courage to commit himself and risk failure.

- With my own financial fiasco, I had a belief that I was financially incompetent. Therefore, despite my apparent caution, I was financially unaccountable. I wanted someone or something to make me rich easily and magically, and I was unconsciously vulnerable to anyone who offered to do this.

These truths can be difficult to tell ourselves. In fact, each of us has created all kinds of dramas and cover stories to keep the truth from ourselves and others.

Please push yourself to get to your truth regarding what has kept you from learning the lessons related to your victimization thus far in your life.

Questions for Friends

If you are having trouble identifying the truths behind your protective behaviors, ask three of your closest friends or family members the following questions:

- What do you perceive are my greatest blind spots—things I don't see or don't see accurately?

- What do your perceive is the truth about me that I may not be conscious of?

- What, in your opinion, have I been avoiding consciously or less than consciously in my life?

Yes, these are big questions, but let your friends and family know what you are up to—breaking old unconscious patterns, becoming personally accountable, and stepping up to live your mission in life—and that you want their support and insight. They will be honored that you asked.

Lessons at Two Levels

Remember that there are lessons to be learned at both the Practical Accountability and Spiritual Accountability levels.

Practical Accountability lessons generally deal with the reality and mechanics of making your way in the world, living with other people, making a living, and raising your kids.

Spiritual Accountability lessons are about why we are here and what our mission is on this planet. (If you are still feeling uncertain about the importance of spiritual lessons, please reread the Spiritual Accountability section in Part 3.)

For example, a man's recurring Victim experiences are all related to being unaccepted or rejected. He develops a variety of beliefs related to those experiences. "Life is hard. To get what I need, I have to do things I'm not proud of." He has difficulty accepting himself because of his actions.

This has caused him to seek approval external to himself by cheating on his wife, compulsively pursuing women he has no interest in just to prove to himself and others that he is significant and desirable.

Consciousness Clue

Adultery is not a cause of relationship break-ups but rather a symptom of a relationship where one or both parties aren't getting their needs met.

In seeking Personal Accountability, he decides that all his spiritual lessons are related to self-acceptance and forgiveness and that his practical lessons are about being transparent and committed in primary relationships. Notice that these lessons are related and connected while not exactly the same. The practical lessons focus on the tangible day-to-day challenges of creating relationships that work, and the spiritual lessons are about the umbrella that has covered most of his experiences. He chooses to believe that, by developing self-acceptance and self-forgiveness, he will be able to interpret and attach meaning to the events in his life.

Carrying forward with this example, the application of the lessons at the Practical Accountability level would include:

- Having completely honest and transparent conversations with his wife.

- Finding a marriage counselor that both he and his wife feel they can work with.

- Consciously and honestly choosing whether he is willing to be committed to transforming their relationship so that it meets both their needs.

The application of the lessons at the Spiritual Accountability level would include:

- Engaging in personal development programs and processes that support self-acceptance and forgiveness.

- Committing to finding a purpose or mission in life.

- Using an affirmation that acknowledges his dual nature of spiritual being and human being along the lines of, "I am an infinite spirit and an imperfect human being. I forgive my human shortcomings."

Remember that being able to articulate the lesson is only the first step in becoming personally accountable. We must put the lessons into action. My standard is that I must be able to articulate at *least* three ways in which I am applying the lessons to my life.

If it is not already clear to you, please note that the application of lessons at one of the levels supports the application of lessons at the other. If he truly forgives himself, it will be much easier to be transparent in his communication. If he discovers and commits to a mission in life, that experience of commitment will support him to commit in other areas of his life, specifically his relationships.

Lesson Themes

To help you knock the dirt off the back of your coin, here are some examples of Victim experiences and possible lessons that could be on the other side of the coin.

Possible Lessons from Abuse

Self-respect

Self-acceptance

Standing up for self

Stopping the cycle

Acting with empathy in support of others

Forgiveness

Conscious partnering and parenting

Possible Lessons from Financial Difficulty

There is more to life than chasing money

Financial responsibility

Focusing on one's unique gifts and resources

Participating

Building financial freedom

Managing or eliminating debt

Contributing to others and the world

Possible Lessons from Infidelity

Commitment

Keeping agreements

Connecting spiritually/intimately outside of sex

Self-acceptance

Forgiveness

Healthy sexual expression

Communication

Internal standards of self-esteem

Abstinence

Fidelity

Possible Lessons from Self-Punishment, Guilt, or Negative Self-Talk

Self-acceptance

Forgiveness

I value myself for who I am, not for what I do

I am a divine child of God/the universe/ the source

Treating myself as I would treat others

Treating others as I would like to be treated

Being a better parent and partner

Using my ability to direct thoughts and energy

Possible Lessons from Theft or Loss

Knowing I am not my possessions

Knowing others are in greater need than I

Forgiveness

Appreciating what I have

Evaluating attachment and detachment

Setting standards of trust

Possible Lessons from Rejection

Knowing I can stand on my own

Self-acceptance

Learning how I want to treat others

Empathizing with others

Being authentic

Realizing I can face and handle conflict

Using and sharing power

Possible Lessons from Being Taken for Granted

I am a human *being*, not a human *doing*

Receiving

Creating relationships with givers instead of takers

Valuing equality in relationships

Asking directly for what I want or need

Possible Lessons from Embarrassment

I am human and perfectly imperfect

Accepting my gifts and challenges

I can laugh at myself, not take myself so seriously

Understanding that others' judgments are more about them than about me

Possible Lessons from Ridicule

Understanding the fears and weaknesses of those who ridicule

Understanding my own fears and weaknesses because I perceive these words and actions as ridicule

Compassion for others who are ridiculed

I can laugh at myself, not take myself so seriously

Possible Lessons from Being Fired

Assessing my contributions honestly

Assessing whether I have chosen the right live-lihood (doing what I am uniquely suited to do versus being motivated by convenience, money, ease, etc.)

Learning leadership skills

Becoming solution-oriented

Risking being heard

Taking a stand

Living up to my ethical standards

Possible Lessons from Divorce

Using authentic communication

Identifying needs in relationships

Giving what someone else wants

Loving (I want for you what you want)

Putting others' needs first

Happiness

Acknowledging and accepting mistakes

Putting my children's needs first

My Own Financial Lessons

Practical Accountability

To learn what Personal Accountability really means and to share that with the world

To be both personally accountable and responsible for the creation and protection of my assets

To focus on *my* unique skills and abilities to create my financial freedom and assets

To focus on my contributions and let the money follow

To focus on the resources that I have, not on what might be easier over there

To be able to say, "My financial security relies on me. I will not hand my money over to someone to 'do it for me.'"

To spend my energy moving toward a vision, rather than overcoming a trauma or difficulty

Spiritual Accountability

My work at Personal Best is not done yet. It is too important to set aside.

I have a major contribution to make to the personal development industry.

My mission in life is to be personally accountable and share my vision of Personal Accountability with the planet.

When I look at my own lessons at both a practical and a spiritual level, they feel right. In the time since this occurred, I have been more creative, more focused on contribution, and clearer about my purpose and mission than ever before in my life.

The tangible results have also been quite astounding to me. My business sales are up over 300 percent, my passive income over 500 percent. I have the largest team in the history of my business. I have created more printed and published material than ever before. The most important part of all of this is that it has happened with a significant sense of ease, flow, and faith. This is not to say that I haven't applied myself, taken significant risks, and worked hard. But my experience of myself is more purposeful, more on track with what matters most, less stressed, less worried, and clearer than I have been in the past.

Avoiding the Spiritual Bypass

On the topic of lessons and their application, it is significant to point out that some people, particularly those who are on a spiritual path, sometimes want to bypass all the other steps and jump straight to Spiritual Accountability. I call this the spiritual bypass.

Often with the spiritual bypass there is simply an acknowledgement of divine participation and an acceptance that "this is what it is." While such a leap certainly supports accepting what is in our lives, I believe it often misses the larger point and potential purpose. The leap does little to discover and attach meaning to an event and even less to integrate and apply its lessons.

Here are my questions for someone who may be making a spiritual bypass:

- What are the choices you made to co-create this result or experience?
- What are the practical lessons?
- What are the ways you are applying those lessons in your life?

In most cases, when a spiritual bypass has been attempted, I am greeted with a deer-in-the-headlights look. I then send my coaching client off to come up with answers for those questions. The result, in most cases, is action, forward motion, and even more meaningful interpretation and application of the spiritual lessons.

Activity – Avoiding the Spiritual Bypass

Choose a significant Victim experience and articulate the lesson(s). No spiritual bypass here!

Here is my Practical Accountability lesson:

How am I applying or how will I apply the lesson?

Here is my Spiritual Accountability lesson:

How am I applying or how will I apply the lesson?

Forgiving Yourself

Sometimes my coaching clients become stuck in their victimization and are unwilling or unable to let go of blame and move to accountability. As a generalization, they are often caught in severe Self-Blame. One of the most powerful tools for self-forgiveness I have found is a simple statement I first heard years ago as a participant in the Personal Best Course:

> "I have always made the best possible choice the instant that I made it with the information that I had."

Now personalize this statement by reading it aloud three times. How does it feel? True? False? Obvious? Ridiculous?

The first time I heard this statement, I thought it was the most ridiculous, obviously false statement I had ever heard. Give me a break. I could list hundreds, perhaps thousands, of stupid choices in my life that I knew better than to make, even as I was making them. A voice inside me was shouting, "No, don't do that. Don't!" Yet, I proceeded to do exactly what I knew intellectually I shouldn't.

For example, my sister, Deb, was diagnosed with dyslexia at an early age. We lived in a small rural town in Saskatchewan, Canada. In those days, there were no such things as teachers' aides or special support programs. There were several grades and one teacher in a single room. So my Mom took it upon herself to tutor Deb. Many of my childhood memories are of Deb studying with Mom. One particular time stands out in my mind. Mom and Deb had worked all weekend preparing for a social studies test. I ran in and out of the house, paying little attention but aware of what they were doing. Sunday evening came, and they were working on a practice test. Mom asked a question and Deb didn't know the answer. But I did. I was seven years younger, and I hadn't done any of the work that Deb had done, and I knew the answer.

I knew that if I said the answer, Deb would be hurt. Now, I should point out that Deb and I did not have any sibling rivalry. We got along great. I loved her dearly and still do, so I did not *want* to hurt her. Yet, even as the thought was in my head "Don't say the answer. You'll hurt Deb," the answer came rushing out of my mouth. The look on Deb's face said everything.

Go back to the statement I asked you to read aloud earlier.

"I have always made the best possible choice the instant that I made it with the information that I had."

That statement does not seem to be accurate, based on my example. Yet, I believe that it is because of the definition of the word "information." Most of us, when we read that statement, interpret the word "information" to mean what we intellectually know or understand. However, "information" means *all* information in all aspects of life. So, consider information to be what you knew or understood about yourself, the world, and relationships—physically, mentally, emotionally, and spiritually—*at the time*.

That changes the meaning of the statement substantially. It provides one of the greatest tools to tell yourself the truth, to evaluate yourself and your life, and, perhaps most important, to *forgive* yourself. What is the point of beating yourself up and feeling bad over what was the best choice you knew how to make at the time?

One way to evaluate such situations in your past is to rate your overall maturity or development at the time on a scale of zero to ten, with zero representing completely unconscious and unaware, and ten being fully developed and mature.

In my example, here is where I was on the scale:

Mentally – 8 I was very sharp for my age and was often told I related and understood like an adult. I had great need and desire to continue to get acceptance and love because of my intellect.

Physically – 6 This did not play any significant role in this choice.

Emotionally – 3 I was immature and at times unsure of myself. I knew at that point that my parents' marriage was troubled, and I wanted approval to assure myself that all would be well. I wanted more than anything for my parents to utter the words "aren't you smart" and be proud of me.

Spiritually – 1 I had no comprehension of spirituality. I attended Sunday school, but that was it.

When I examine the "information" that I had when I made that choice, it is abundantly clear to me that I did, in fact, make the best possible choice I knew how to make with the information I had the instant that I made it.

Activity – Forgiving Yourself

Describe a decision that you made in the past that you continue to blame yourself for and that you would like to forgive yourself for.

Rate your maturity in each of the following 4 areas on a scale of 0–10, and write a line or two about the needs that were being fulfilled in each area when you made that choice.

Mentally 0 1 2 3 4 5 6 7 8 9 10

The needs being fulfilled were:

Emotionally 0 1 2 3 4 5 6 7 8 9 10

The needs being fulfilled were:

Physically 0 1 2 3 4 5 6 7 8 9 10

The needs being fulfilled were:

Spiritually 0 1 2 3 4 5 6 7 8 9 10

The needs being fulfilled were:

Adapt the following statement to your particular choice, write it down, and then read it out loud.

I, _____, acknowledge and accept that the choice I made to

_____

_____

was the best choice I knew how to make at the time with the information I had, mentally, emotionally, physically, and spiritually. I forgive myself completely.

Forgiving Others

In her book, *Unconditional Love and Forgiveness*, Edith Stauffer says, "Forgiveness is a decision not to hurt ourselves for the wrongs done by others, or other circumstances. It is a decision to re-enter the flow of life." Colin

C. Tipping, author of *Radical Forgiveness*, believes that, "*Radical Forgiveness* occurs simply as a consequence of our opening up to the possibility that everything happens for a reason, and there are no mistakes. If we could see the spiritual big picture (which we cannot), we would understand that the situation was Divinely guided and happened not to us, but for us...our Higher Selves actually called forth the experience for our healing and our spiritual growth."

Using the "Pattern Interrupt"

The movie *What the Bleep Do We Know!?* illustrates one of the best explanations of what a "pattern interrupt" is and why it is important in creating any change. (You can find out much more about the significance of pattern interrupts by researching NLP or Neuro-Linguistic Programming.) I will do my best to summarize the main points.

In each of our brains there are millions and millions of neurons. They are something like fingers that have receptors and receivers on them. These neurons link together to create a thought or a memory so we can understand an idea. A series of neurons that are wired together are called a *neural net* or a *neural pathway*.

If you were to think about your most significant Victim experience, it would trigger exactly the same neurons that have been wired together since the original event occurred. (I would hope that statement is no longer 100 percent true. If you have read this entire book and done the activities, new neural pathways should fire as well, but you get the point.)

Every time a neural pathway is used, it becomes stronger. As the movie says, "Neurons that fire together wire together." One of the reasons it can be difficult to break old Victim patterns is that once a triggering thought, perception, or experience occurs, a racing cascade of neurons starts to fire along the established neural net.

You have all had that experience. You are going along and things are great. Then something happens that triggers a thought or memory, and wham! Suddenly you feel down, agitated, annoyed, or sad. At times you cannot shake that thought or memory. What has just occurred is the conscious or unconscious triggering of an old and powerful neural network. As these neurons fired, they gave the signal to your pituitary gland to release the neuropeptides that match the emotions you have linked to that memory or experience.

So, if your brain is literally wired to think the same thoughts using the same neural networks, what can you do about it? One of the most powerful and simple approaches is to use *pattern interrupts.*

And what is a pattern interrupt? Anything that interrupts and keeps the neural net from firing in the same way that it always has. Ideally, the pattern interrupt also creates a new, more supportive and powerful neural network. From that perspective, this entire book is designed to help you interrupt the old Victim-framed networks and use them to establish new supportive neural networks grounded in Personal Accountability, evolution, and mission. (For more information about this, refer to Anthony Robbins' *Awaken the Giant Within.*)

One of the difficult things about implementing pattern interrupts is that we are so conditioned to the old networks firing that we are mainly unconscious of it. A perfect example of this is what happens when I use the following technique in my seminars. I ask participants to use accountable language—*I, me,* and *my.* Each time they say *you, we,* or *everyone,* and I believe that they are talking about themselves, I point at my chest as a cue to them to shift their language. This works for most people. However, there are those for whom I must use a verbal pattern interrupt, asking them, "Who? Me or you?" There are cases where, even after several days, a verbal pattern interrupt is necessary. That is how powerful a neural network can be. A key to using pattern interrupts successfully is to enlist the support of the people in your life. They are often able to notice your patterns long before you can.

Here are some pattern interrupts you can use.

Stop, Look, and Choose

This is an interrupt that we teach in Personal Best Level One, Truth Revealed. It is simple and powerful. When you find yourself in any negative pattern or Victim framing, you can say aloud (or to yourself):

> **Stop** this unconscious automatic reaction; stop referencing the past and projecting it on the present.

> **Look** at what is really going on, right here, right now. Look at the opportunity that presents itself. Look at what the real choices are in this moment.

> **Choose** a response that is congruent with who you want to be, what you want to do, and what you want to have in your life.

Stop, Look, and Choose, as simple as it sounds, is a foundational tool that will support you in developing your consciousness. As you practice, you'll improve your ability to interrupt negative patterns. Over time, you will catch yourself earlier and earlier, sometimes even before the reaction actually happens.

The Elastic Band

I like this one for its simplicity, even though some people can find a way to misuse it. Slip an elastic band around your wrist. Each time you want to interrupt Victim thinking or framing, snap the elastic and redirect your thoughts and energy. Warning: If you have strong Self-Blame Victim tendencies, be careful that the elastic is not just one more way to beat yourself up.

The elastic snap is just a physical shock to interrupt the initial pattern. You must then consciously redirect your energy. To be sure that you keep a positive attachment to the process, say "Thank you for the reminder" to yourself as you build your new neural pathway.

Cartoon by Dr. Brian Read, presented to me after he attended one of my accountability intensive weekends.

HISTORICAL VIGNETTES: THE PROTOTYPE "®ACCOUNTABILITY ELASTIC"

Affirmations

Much has been written about affirmations over the years. There could hardly be more difference of opinion about which techniques work or don't work. I am not going to get into debating the details. I'll just tell you I use affirmations, I've used them for fifteen years, and I have found a way that is powerful for me. I believe that my consistency with my affirmations is one of the primary ways I learned to direct my energy and my will.

Affirmations can work at several levels:

- Affirmations as simple reminders
- Affirmations as triggers, a method to surface your issues
- Affirmations as programming tools

All of them support the creation of new neural pathways.

Affirmations as Reminders

In their simplest form, affirmations that are used consistently—let's say every morning and evening—are reminders to our consciousness. They build awareness of what we want and don't want in our lives. We must have this foundation to use pattern interrupts effectively.

If, for example, one of my affirmations is, "I, Jay, exercise five times a week. It clears my mind and multiplies my energy." At a reminder level, each time I do this affirmation, I review how many times I have or have not been physically active, and I acknowledge my success or plan for any adjustments. Each time I do this, I am reinforcing a new neural network that is vital to my long-term health and happiness.

Do not underestimate the power of reminders that are congruent to your purpose. They work.

Affirmations as Triggers

Using affirmations as a method to surface your issues is underrated and often not even considered. The truth is that most people who have been on a consciousness or spiritual journey have at least tried affirmations. Most people do not use them for the long haul. I believe that people quit for two reasons.

First, they may believe that they don't work. I can't tell you how many times I've heard, "I did affirmations for six months, but they didn't work, so I quit." My question is always, "How many times in your life do you think that your limiting beliefs have been reinforced, consciously or less than consciously?" I usually get a response ranging from hundreds of thousands to millions. Yet people want affirmations to "work" after 200 or 400 tries. While that would be nice, it is not all that likely. Will 200 to 400 times help? They will lay the foundation for an entirely new neural network, but that network must be used and strengthened over and over. Ultimately, it will become strong enough to unwire the old negative Victim network. Affirmations require both patience and persistence.

A second reason that people quit is that affirmations can trigger discomfort, resistance, and cognitive dissonance. At first glance, all these unpleasant experiences seem to justify stopping.

The alternative I suggest is to continue the affirmations and add another element to your routine. Ask yourself, "Is there anything else besides conscious beliefs that is reacting against my affirmations? Is there another source for my discomfort?" Your answer can be incredibly enlightening and provide insights you may never have imagined. You can compare this process to panning for gold. You need to get some sediment into the pan and then, with continued motion, you release the unnecessary sand, dirt, and pebbles to reveal the heavier shiny nuggets that make it all worthwhile. Don't be afraid to stir up the sediment. If you are feeling uncomfortable, take it as a sign that there is a nugget lurking under those affirmations. You just need to keep asking, "What beliefs are creating these feelings?"

Affirmations as Programming Tools

This is where things get interesting. I remember reading one of the grandfathers of all personal development books, *Psychocybernetics* by Dr. Maxwell Maltz. He wrote about how the mind cannot tell the difference between something that has actually happened and something that is vividly imagined. I read that over and over, trying to integrate the implications of that statement. If it were true, then what power each of us would have between our ears!

Over the years, a tremendous amount of research has supported that statement. So how do we get this amazing truth working for us? Simply by adding fully associated visualizations to our pattern interrupt affirmations.

Here is the method I use for blending affirmations and visualizations. Primarily, I listen to my affirmations on my iPod. When I record them, I say the affirmation, then pause for five or ten seconds so I have time to visualize this experience or result in my life with great feeling. Then I say the affirmation again. I find this process far more powerful than just saying the words as I did when I first started.

A key point to the visualization is, if possible, to bring to mind an experience in your life where what you are affirming has actually happened. Use that image to start with. If you don't have such an experience in your life, then create that situation in your imagination. When you do this, be very specific. *Feel* the feelings you associate with this experience and visualize it in the first person. See the scene through your own eyes. Don't watch yourself as if you were on television.

> **Affirmation:** I, _____, choose to be accountable and to apply my lessons that support me in fulfilling my life mission.

Visualization: Vividly recall a situation where you chose to be accountable, identify the lesson, and see yourself applying that lesson. Link it to what you believe your mission to be.

For me, it is easy to use my financial fiasco to recall its lessons and to see myself applying those lessons. One of my favorites is seeing myself writing this book and then flashing forward to imagining Oprah holding the book and introducing me on her show. I then see people all over the planet changing their lives for the better by applying the concepts of Personal Accountability. I feel pride for seeing the idea through to completion. I feel gratitude for my life and the people in it who support me. Above all, I experience the emotion that I have yet to name, but which is best described as the *freedom* of Personal Accountability.

Let's tie this basic affirmation process back to when and how to use affirmations as pattern interrupts. As I said, when I first began using affirmations, I repeated them twice a day. First thing in the morning, before all the filters of the conscious mind kick in, and when I have more direct access to the subconscious mind, I'd repeat my affirmations. Then, last thing at night, I would direct my subconscious to reflect on what I intended to create in my life.

This worked out very well, but I soon found another powerful use. Anytime I realized I was feeling down, confused, victimized, or stuck in a negative or limiting emotion, I would also do my affirmations. They quickly became my most powerful pattern interrupt.

Commit to a structure for using your affirmations. This will serve and support you over the long haul. Keep your affirmations handy for whenever you need to change your state, redirect your energy, and become personally accountable.

⌕ **Consciousness Clue**

Have you ever awakened to a song on your clock radio and then had that song "stuck" in your head for the rest of the day, even if you did not particularly like the song? You have experienced why it's valuable to do your affirmations first thing in the morning before all the filters of your fully awakened conscious mind are in place.

One of my early motivations for putting my affirmations on my iPod was that I wanted to be able to do my workout and my affirmations simultaneously as a time saver. It certainly was, and for many years I have combined the two. Now, here is the interesting part. I have created a neural network that links the experiences together. For example, if I am exercising without listening to my iPod, my brain *automatically* starts doing my affirmations. On the other hand, if I am doing my affirmations as a pattern interrupt or in preparation for a presentation, I suddenly feel compelled to run or do something physical. These two very supportive behaviors have intertwined their neural networks so that one behavior triggers another. This is a nice transition to our next pattern interrupt.

Physical Activity

I do not want to become one of those people who keep telling you to exercise. You already know the health benefits. You know how you feel when you do, and you know how much fun it can be if you do something that you love. It's interesting that, with all this awareness, many are becoming more sedentary, so much so that childhood obesity is considered an epidemic in North America. As an old business partner of mine used to say, "To know and not to do is not quite yet to know." But I digress.

Physical activity as a pattern interrupt is powerful because it affects our physiology and brain. Sustained physical activity creates increased blood flow, sending much-needed oxygen to the brain and stimulating the immune system. You can then frame this pleasurable sensation as a message to your belief system that, "I love and respect myself. I take care of myself." If you have issues with self-acceptance, self-confidence, or self-esteem, commit to using physical activity as part of a self-care routine and as a pattern interrupt for your Victim thoughts and framing.

Powerful Questions

I am going to focus on one more powerful pattern interrupt and then simply give you a list to research, try out, and discover what is going to work for you.

I believe that the quality of people's lives is directly linked to the quality of the questions they ask. "Successful people ask better questions," notes Tony Robbins, "and as a result, they get better answers." In fact, Victim framing and many Victim thoughts start with questions like:

- Why does this always happen to me?
- Why don't they respect my wishes?
- Why is this so hard?
- Why are people so stupid?

Whew! I get depressed just typing those questions. It is amazing how quickly a person asking such questions will become drained and draining.

Clearly these are *not* powerful personally accountable questions, and, as a generalization, any question that starts with a "why" is not as powerful as a question reframed to start with a "what" or a "how."

The word "why" implies that there is something wrong with the way things are. Often you have already evaluated the situation and decided that you want someone else to change. Asking "why" can generate resistance, and resistance is a first cousin to victimization.

Powerful questions starting with "how" or "what" are fantastic pattern interrupts and can work like a charm. Every time you hear yourself asking a Victim-framed "why" question, stop and reframe it with a "how" or "what."

Susan Piver, author of *The Hard Questions for an Authentic Life*, says, "Asking a question can be a sacred act. A real question assumes a dialogue, a link to the source from which answers come. Asking a question is a simple, profound way of initiating a relationship with the energies and powers around and within you." Let's try it.

Why does this always happen to me?
becomes
What could I learn from this recurring pattern?

Why don't they respect my wishes?
becomes
How can I create agreements that are honored?

Why is this so hard?
becomes
What is so difficult about this for me, and how can I create some support?

Why are people so stupid?
becomes
How am I failing to communicate? What am I not understanding?

The difference in the power of the questions is immediately apparent. What is less apparent is the long-term influence of this particular pattern interrupt. You learn that better questions can provide the answers to all your issues.

There are an unlimited number of pattern interrupts. It really does not matter so much which ones you choose to use. What matters is that you are clear on the reason you are using pattern interrupts. You are intervening and stopping the old neural network that reinforces negative feelings, victimization, and powerlessness. Each time you interrupt the firing of those neurons and redirect your mind to thoughts grounded in Personal Accountability, the old neural pathways weaken. The new ones get stronger until ultimately you will have a series of neural networks that fire consistently and automatically, directing your focus and energy to what you control and have significant influence over.

Activity – Researching Pattern Interrupts

Go on the Internet and research some or all of the pattern interrupt methods listed below. Commit to using three from my suggestions above or your research. (I like using three to stay vigilant as I am bringing my consciousness to bear on a new concept or life area.)

Breath Work

Meditation

NLP (Neuro-Linguistic Programming)

Emotional Freedom Technique

Brain Gym (Edu K or Educational Kinesiology)

Consciousness Clue

When committing to using pattern interrupts, one of the greatest supports is to get a buddy to point out what you don't notice yourself (and there will be lots of things you don't notice). We all need that external, objective point of view to interrupt our habitual ways of being.

Your Most Powerful Tool

Time and again throughout this book you have read "direct and focus your energy on what you can control and influence." I believe this is one of the most powerful capabilities we humans have, yet we are rarely taught how to use it. There are many time-honored approaches to directing our energy and our will such as meditation, martial arts, prayer, coaching, mentoring by a guru, psychotherapy, and the true mastery of anything—a sport, a musical instrument, our own belief systems. The list could go on and on. Let's be frank. Most of these techniques require time and effort, but our quick-fix society rarely is willing to pay the price. We require instant answers, a magic pill, or a five-minute process to get the results we want.

I promise you no quick or easy answer, but I will give you a few techniques that will support you as you direct your energy and will to Personal Accountability and to what you control.

Dr. Victor E. Frankl spent three years in Hitler's prison camps during World War II. He observed in his book, *Man's Search for Meaning*, that even the extraordinarily degrading and dehumanizing surroundings could not deprive some captives of their most precious gift.

> The experiences of [concentration] camp life show that man does have a choice of action...Man can preserve a vestige of spiritual freedom, of independence of mind, even in such terrible conditions of psychic and physical stress...

> Everything can be taken from a man, but one thing: the last of the human freedoms—to choose one's attitude in any given set of circumstances, to choose one's own way.

There were always choices to make. Every day, every hour, offered the opportunity to make a decision, a decision which determined whether you would or would not submit to those powers which threatened to rob you of your very self, your inner freedom; which determined whether or not you would become the plaything of circumstance, renouncing freedom and dignity to become molded into the form of the typical inmate...The last inner freedom cannot be lost.

Dr. Frankl is talking about choosing what you think, feel, and do in any situation. Think for a moment what it would take to choose your feelings in the midst of the horror and death of a concentration camp. Most of us are not able to do so while enjoying the most freedom, the most abundance, and the easiest life that has ever existed on the planet. Let's make sure this lack of choice doesn't apply to *you.*

At the beginning of this book, I promised you simple, straightforward ways to become more personally accountable. If you have been doing the activities along the way, you have discovered many of them already. However, I'm going to help you now with a summary sheet of questions to ask yourself, each tailored to the particular levels of victimhood or accountability where you are now. These questions will help you to deal with your victimization and to frame your experiences from the perspective of Personal Accountability. Let's follow the levels of victimization, as shown on the Evolution of Personal Accountability chart on the next page.

The Evolution of Personal Accountability

Personal Accountability: A framing device that eliminates blame of self and others, providing the power of choice, participation, and co-creation of the experiences and results in our lives, real or imagined.

Spiritual Accountability

I am a Spiritual Being having a human experience. My purpose here is to experience myself, remember who I am, and evolve at a spiritual level. I co-create everything based on this. I even choose my parents, and I choose the time, place, and method of my death through every choice I make in my entire life.

Practical Accountability

I co-create my results and experiences in life. I focus on my choices without blame. There is a lesson in everything, and I choose to find it.

Emotional-Response Accountability

I cannot always control or influence the events in my life, but I always have a choice about how I will feel about them. I respond without blame.

Self-Righteous Victim

I cannot always control or influence the events in my life, but I always have choices about how I will feel about them and how I will respond. I can do this and still blame others, myself, the world, and circumstances for my life.

Self-Blame Victim

I made bad or stupid choices. My life is my fault. There is something wrong with me. I am powerless to influence my life, world, and future.

External-Blame Victim

Someone, something external to me, has done me wrong. If this had not happened, then my life would be better. They did it to me, and there is nothing I can do about it. I am powerless to influence my life, world, and future.

Victimization: A frame of reference, experience, or belief (real or imagined, internal or external) involving blame that removes or distances power, choice, and action. Consciously or unconsciously accepting and believing that you are a Victim.

External-Blame Victim

- Am I willing to waste my life and my energy blaming others for this?
- Do I want to continue draining myself and others of energy, love, and support?
- What are my payoffs for choosing to blame others and being powerless?
- What beliefs am I protecting or reinforcing by choosing to blame others and being powerless?
- How can I truly release blame to experience Personal Accountability?
- What level of Personal Accountability will best assist me to deal with this situation?

Self-Blame Victim

- Am I willing to waste my life and my energy blaming myself for this?
- Do I want to continue draining myself and others of energy, love and support?
- What are my payoffs for choosing to punish or diminish myself?
- What beliefs am I protecting or reinforcing by choosing to punish or diminish myself?
- How can I truly forgive myself to release blame and experience Personal Accountability?
- What level of Personal Accountability will best assist me to deal with this situation?

Self-Righteous Victim

- What are my payoffs for choosing this Victim framing?
- What is blocking me from releasing blame in this circumstance?
- What beliefs am I protecting or reinforcing by choosing this Victim framing?
- Am I willing to waste my life and my energy blaming myself or others for this?
- Do I want to continue draining myself and others of energy, love, and support?
- How can I truly forgive myself or others so I can release blame and experience Personal Accountability?
- What level of Personal Accountability will best assist me to deal with this situation?

The previous questions were designed to assist you in moving from Victim to Personal Accountability. The following questions will help you be clear and grounded as you transition between the three levels of Personal Accountability.

Emotional-Response Accountability

- How can I focus my energy and will on what I can control?
- What are my real choices in this situation?
- What will I choose to think?
- What will I choose to feel?
- What will I choose to do?

Practical Accountability

- Without blaming myself (or anyone else), what are the choices I made to co-create this experience or result?

- What are my *specific* payoffs for being a Victim? (Remember that the three general categories are recognition, excuses—always true for victimization—and deception.) Can I get those needs met in a more healthy and direct manner by applying the remedies?

- What specific beliefs are being reinforced? What am I getting to be right about? How can I take a consciously-designed risk to counterbalance or release old limiting beliefs?

- Is this part of a recurring pattern? If so, how does it fit the pattern?

- What can I learn from this experience? What are my practical lessons?

- How can I apply the lesson or lessons in at least three specific ways in my life?

Spiritual Accountability

- To ensure this is not a spiritual bypass, am I clear about the choices I made to co-create this result or experience? Am I clear about the Practical Accountability lesson? Can I articulate how I am applying those lessons? If not, answer all of these questions *before* proceeding.

- What is the deeper spiritual meaning in this experience? What might be the spiritual lesson?

- What clues might this experience have for me about my life mission?

- How can I use this experience to live my mission more fully and consciously?

Learn to Look at Context

What is context? A dictionary definition is "the circumstances or events that form the environment within which something exists or takes place."

I generally think of context as a container, something that holds something else. A coffee cup is a container (or context) that holds coffee, cream, and sugar (content). What I like about this image is that obviously the coffee cup, to a great extent, limits and influences the nature of the content.

If you have an eight-ounce coffee cup, how much coffee can you carry around in it? Eight ounces or fewer. If you wanted to transport a gallon of liquid (coffee or anything else) at one time, you would need a larger container or context.

Note that even calling the cup a "coffee cup" places some limitations upon its use and abilities. What if it was just a container? Does that change its usefulness? If you wanted to transport eight ounces of honey bees or helium, you'd need a container of a different size and shape.

The point of this example is simple. Recognize that you, as a human being, are also a context, a container that is defined by your beliefs.

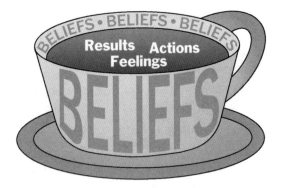

Your context or container can hold only the content that your belief system allows, in this case your results, actions, and feelings.

If you believe that you cannot ask directly for the love, support, and attention that you need, then you will be locked into actions that attempt to get your needs met in an indirect way. You transform yourself into a Victim to get payoffs and protections as you try to fulfill your needs and reinforce your belief (your context) that you cannot ask directly for the love, support, and attention that you need.

Consciousness Clue

You have exactly the results in your life that your context allows, no more and no less. To identify your beliefs, examine your results. "Based on (insert results), I must believe..." For example, "Based on my being brokenhearted and lonely, I must believe that primary relationships don't work."

Our society is taught to focus on the *content* of our lives instead of the *context.* For example, how many of you have needed more money at some point in your life? To achieve this, you may have asked for a raise, changed to a higher-paying job, or taken a second job. These actions make perfect sense if you are focusing on *content* only. Let's take it further. How many of you have raised your income and still been financially stretched? Research says that for most people, the more we earn, the more we spend. Increased income does not necessarily improve our financial situations. On the one hand, this is simply crazy. On the other hand, it makes perfect sense. The *context* for most people in a credit-based economy is to spend just a little more than they make.

I believe the old saying "the more things change, the more they stay the same" applies to the phenomenon of our society focusing on *content*. We can easily stir up the *content* in our container, and it looks like things are changing. Yet, if we stop stirring momentarily, we soon find that things are not that different at all.

So, how do you really manifest genuine change? The answer is to shift your focus to your *context*. Begin to understand the size of your container. What are the beliefs that determine the size of your *context* and how does that influence your results (or lack thereof)? By considering *context*, you will often see your *content* more honestly and accurately as well. The perspective of context shifts actions and solutions toward addressing the source of your issues.

If we go back to the money example, it is clear that if the operating context is to spend 102% of what we earn, then additional income *won't make any difference*. In fact, another job will just get you into debt faster. Yikes!

Think that through. The solution that seems so apparent at the content level actually compounds the issue in reality. Instead of accumulating $1,000 debt per year at $50,000 income, you go $2,000 into the hole each year on a $100,000 income.

By viewing the issue from a *context* perspective, we begin to see that the issue is not so much about how much money we are earning but how much money we are spending. This issue must be addressed before extra income can make a positive difference.

How could you address finances from the context perspective? The first thing *I* would start with is becoming clear about my beliefs about money and possessions and my beliefs about safety and security. I would see what beliefs are limiting my experience of being satisfied and comfortable with my finances.

One starting point might be this question:

Based on the result of spending more money than I earn, what must I believe about money, debt, financial responsibility, and financial freedom?

Quick brainstorming may reveal answers like these:

- I have to work hard to succeed. (You will always have a good reason to work hard if you are in debt.)
- Financial freedom is for rich people, not me.
- I am a working man, therefore I work.
- I have to keep up appearances and look successful.
- I don't have to take care of my finances. I will get an inheritance (or win the lottery).
- I deserve to reward myself with gifts and things. I work *hard*.
- Everyone has debt. That's how you buy things.
- I can't live on $_____ a year!
- If I can make the minimum payments, then I can afford it.
- I *need* to go out for lunch every day (get a new car every three years, take annual holidays—fill in your "needs.")
- It is my partner's job to take care of the money.
- There is never enough money to save anything.
- I *would* save money if there was ever any left at the end of the month.

Each of these statements reveals beliefs about money and power. To shift long-term financial results, it is necessary to address context and the beliefs that limit earning capacity and underlie spending habits. Only when these are addressed will increasing income change the financial situation.

Consciousness Clue

In our society money is viewed as power and victimization is also related to power or, more accurately, lack of power. Therefore, it is no surprise that people with Victim issues often have financial issues as well. They go hand-in-hand! If you want to expand your context for an abundance of money, expand your context of Personal Accountability. Solutions to your money issues will follow.

To become personally accountable, acknowledge the content in your life, but don't get sucked into believing this is all that matters. Your content (results, feelings, and actions) are simply reflections or feedback to you about your context (your beliefs).

This whole book has been nothing more than tools, techniques, and approaches, preparing you to say, "Hmmm, based on my results, what do I believe and what can I learn that will expand my context?"

Identifying Your Life Mission

You have read the book, done the activities, and you are now more personally accountable. With your current understanding, you recognize that it is possible— just possible—that your recurring Victim experiences have been co-created by you and the Universe, God, or

Source (however you want to think about the supreme power). Yes or no?

I believe that, intuitively, you believe the answer is "yes." Your rational mind may want to debate it, but part of you is acknowledging, "This must be true."

The reason I say this is that in the Personal Freedom Program, every time I ask, "What if your recurring Victim experiences are your single greatest clue to your life mission?" I am greeted with a stunned look. "Huh?"

It's as though the seminar participants had just been hit on the head. Often there is an almost magical pause—you know, one of those moments when time seems to stop. Then several people say at the same time, "Could you repeat that, please?"

I interpret that reaction as the higher part of ourselves resonating with a truth that our lower self cannot yet comprehend or integrate.

This brings us to the final and most important Activity of this book: the Life Mission worksheet. This takes all the individual concepts we have covered and weaves them together into a tool that provides an answer to one of the biggest questions of life. The depth of your answer depends upon your willingness, honesty and comprehension.

As you fill out the worksheet, don't agonize. There are no right or wrong answers. All you are doing is noticing your patterns, needs, and motivations, and interpreting them all in a meaningful manner.

First, read the sample worksheet, beginning on the opposite page, that uses my own financial fiasco—the example that I have used throughout this book.

Sample Activity – *My* Life Mission Worksheet

My most significant recurring victimization experience is:

> *Investing my $$ in business ventures where I do not have direct control and where I abdicate both accountability and responsibility, hoping that someone will do it for me. This can result in great financial loss.*

The feelings that these experiences trigger in me are:

> *Stupidity, incompetence, a crisis to overcome, sadness.*

My specific payoffs for these recurring experiences are:

> *I feel proud and strong when I overcome. It keeps me busy recovering instead of creating and looking forward. By failing, I don't have to or can't live my big dream, arousing sympathy in others.*

The specific beliefs that are being protected or reinforced are:

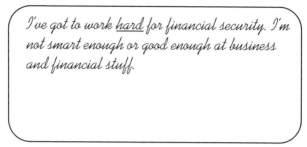

> *I've got to work __hard__ for financial security. I'm not smart enough or good enough at business and financial stuff.*

The lesson that I have been unwilling or unable to learn up to this point is: (If you are having trouble with this question, refer to your lessons from both Practical Accountability and Spiritual Accountability.)

> *That I have unique gifts in learning, facilitating, teaching, and supporting myself and others to wake up—yet I have looked elsewhere for someone and something else to create my financial freedom.*

The reason I have been unable or unwilling to learn this lesson up to this point is:

> *I have been financially unaccountable because I wanted someone or something else to do it for me, easily and magically. I have had a belief that I am financially incompetent, so someone else can do it better than I can, and I will happily let them.*

If I were actually to apply this lesson, how would my life be different?

I would become financially accountable, focus my time and energy exclusively on developing my gifts, skills, resources, and abilities and on monetizing them effectively and contributing to the maximum number of people possible.
I would write a book such as this.

Restate as a mission statement the lesson/s from your recurring experiences of being a Victim.

My mission is to live passionately, positively, and abundantly—manifesting freedom through Personal Accountability in all areas of my life and the lives of others.

Describe how this mission will keep you grounded and accountable:

It will provide a framework and a purpose because it focuses my energy and will on being personally accountable.

Agreement with self—I commit to consciously living my mission by:

> *Continuing to refine, develop, and deliver my seminars.*
>
> *Hiring and training support and staff in all areas of my life and business to create time and space for creation.*
>
> *Continuing to write and hire support for the editing and completion of the book.*
>
> *Have the book completed by December 31, 2006.*

Now starting at the beginning of the worksheet below, answer each question as honestly and as completely as you can. Remember, there is no pressure. This is an exploration, not a test. (NOTE: You can download full-size worksheets from the Free Resources page at www.personalbestseminars.com/free-resources.php)

Activity – *Your* Life Mission Worksheet

My most significant recurring victimization experience is:

The feelings that these experiences trigger in me are:

My specific payoffs for these recurring experiences are:

The specific beliefs that are being protected or reinforced are:

The lesson that I have been unwilling or unable to learn up to this point is: (If you are having trouble with this question, refer to your lessons from both Practical Accountability and Spiritual Accountability.)

The reason I have been unable or unwilling to learn this lesson up to this point is:

If I were actually to apply this lesson, how would my life be different?

Restate as a mission statement the lesson/s from your recurring experiences of being a Victim.

Describe how this mission will keep you grounded and accountable:

Agreement with self—I commit to consciously living my mission by:

Once you are finished, I strongly recommend that you share your mission and how you are going to live it with the significant people in your life. You can also communicate online with other people working on their missions by using the discussion board linked from the Free Resources page at

www.personalbestseminars.com/free-resources.php

Awareness Is Not Enough

If it is not already clear to you, I am a huge proponent of application and follow-through. In these last pages, I want to encourage you to honestly assess yourself and your participation while reading this book. Did you read the entire book or just the parts that intrigued or interested you? Did you do all the activities? Did you complete the mission worksheet?

Awareness is not enough. Application is required. Your participation in this book is a direct mirror of your desire and willingness to be personally accountable. Based on results, rate your desire and willingness. Understanding the pain and cost of Victim framing, are you really prepared to continue the Victim patterns that exist in your life?

Remember that I suggested you use this book as both a workbook and a textbook. As a workbook because you have filled in the Activities. As a textbook because you can make notes and highlight sections that are significant to you. Another characteristic of a textbook is that it is studied over and over until the knowledge and lessons become integrated.

If you have only skimmed this book, if you have read it and agreed intellectually with the ideas but have not yet applied the concepts specifically to you and your life, please go back. Do the work. You will be rewarded beyond measure. It will positively influence the rest of your life. I'll get off my soapbox in a moment, but I am making a point of this for several reasons:

- As a facilitator, I know that homework assignments are completed less than half the time.

- When people have lived their lives within a Victim frame of reference, they are scared that their needs will not be met if another way is tried. Your belief system can consciously or unconsciously sabotage you, keeping you from taking the action necessary to move past being a Victim.

- I know what my life is like from a personally accountable perspective. It is peaceful, meaningful, in flow, accepting, and loving toward myself and others. I wish that for you. I wish that for everyone.

The following section is an example of the application of my mission, which is to live passionately, positively, and abundantly—manifesting freedom through Personal Accountability in all areas of my life and the lives of others.

Living My Mission

All my life, I have been drawn to Africa. Something in my soul burns when I see the starvation, illness, and general hardship that exist upon that continent. Over the years, I have sent money, sponsored children, and supported famine relief but, in truth, it felt empty. I still felt powerless against what I believe to be nothing less than a crime against humanity.

If that seems like an exaggeration, consider that for decades we have had the food production capacity to feed the planet, yet we choose not to. Third-world governments cannot invest in the infrastructure needed because, in many cases, they are struggling under massive debt to the first world. I really believe that the primary reason we do not do enough to help is that the problem is just too far away. Out of sight, out of mind. But what if it were closer?

Imagine your next-door neighbors starving, their children on the front lawn with distended bellies and bones nearly poking through their skin. You pull into your driveway in your brand new car, bringing home your healthy, well-fed (even overfed) children. As your well-dressed, slightly plump kids get out of the car, you shield their eyes and tell them there is not much they can do. It is best to hurry into the house where supper and a new toy await them. You all run inside, lock the door, close the blinds, and turn on the electric fence so the neighbors can't try to steal food from your garden—which you have not tended particularly well because you have been too busy fighting with the family across the street who knocked down one of your lawn ornaments.

Could you do it? I know *I* couldn't walk past a starving child on my street. Yet, I have done it a thousand times by changing the channel when appeals for contributions are broadcast. Our society does it everyday, keeping our heads in the sand, hiding out at the mall, shopping for trinkets and clothes we don't need while over a billion people battle for enough food to stay alive.

For me, I think that in the past I was left powerless by my belief that there was nothing I could really do that would make any difference. The issue is systemic. Sending money is like throwing good money after bad. The countries themselves are under unsustainable debt loads. They are killing themselves in tribal and civil wars anyway. The number of people suffering from AIDS alone will wipe out millions over the next twenty years. How can my little pittance of money make any sort of difference at all?

These myths and many others were dispelled for me in an amazing book, *The End of Poverty*, by Jeffrey D. Sachs. If you have ever wondered what can be done about poverty and world hunger, this is a must-read. It was through this book that I discovered the Millennium Project.

The United Nations Millennium Project

The premise of the huge, multilevel United Nations Millennium Project (www.unmillenniumproject.org) is that extreme poverty on our planet threatens us all by causing instability, disease, and the unnecessary suffering and deaths of millions of people. Yet, such poverty can be brought to a close by our generation!

I was especially excited by one facet, the Millennium Village Project, which makes immediate changes in the lives of individuals. I will summarize what I love about its simple, hands-on ideas and why I have chosen to support it.

The objective is to develop self-sustaining communities by providing technology, training, and investment, rather than a handout. The work started with a dozen "research" villages (now expanded to 78), located in ten African countries: Ethiopia, Ghana, Kenya, Malawi, Mali, Nigeria, Rwanda, Senegal, Tanzania, and Uganda. The locations were chosen as hunger "hotspots," often accompanied by a high level of disease, lack of access to medical care, and a severe lack of infrastructure. Each had to be in a reasonably peaceful nation governed by an accountable government, and located in districts where non-governmental or international donor organizations have been able to work successfully.

The Millennium Village Project focuses on strategic implementations of specific interventions for each village. Some areas of focus are:

Agricultural and agro-forestry techniques dramatically increase farm production while enhancing the environment.

Essential health services provide critical, life-saving medicines and raise productivity. Vitamin and mineral supplements tackle malnutrition and make children stronger.

Burdens on women are relieved by targeted investments, improved access to water and fuel wood, accessible clinics, mills for grain, and trucking and ambulance services.

Free, daily, school lunches using locally produced food support children's nutrition, learning capacity, and school attendance.

Access to anti-retroviral medicines keeps people with HIV/AIDS alive in poor countries, just as it does in rich ones.

Sleeping under an insecticide-treated bed net prevents children from getting malaria, and immunizations will lower the incidence of TB.

Innovative off-grid energy, water, and information technologies not only bring safe water and energy, but save many hours previously spent each day collecting firewood and water.

One of the key premises is that if all the countries of the developed world would contribute seven-tenths of 1 percent of their gross domestic product—a pittance by any standard—we could end world hunger.

I have resolved to be personally accountable for my desire to contribute in a meaningful manner. My resolution is fourfold:

- I am choosing a specific village to support to self-sufficiency. This assists me to direct my thoughts, energy, and actions to a specific goal where I will see results.

- I have committed to continuing my support there long term, a minimum of five years or until the Millennium Project directs its energies to another village because this one has become self-sustaining.

- I am doing what the Millennium Project asks of our government, committing .7 percent of my gross sales of this book, of the income of my company, Personal Best Seminars Inc., and any other personal income for a minimum of five years.

- I am inviting you—as a reader, as a *have* in a world of *have-nots*, as a citizen of planet Earth— to make the same pledge. The .7 percent solution would hardly be felt by most of you. If you earn $100,000 a year, it is only $700, less than $60 a month. Many of you spend more at Starbucks or on parking meters. If you choose to do this, you can make your pledge to the Millennium Project (www.millenniumpromise.org) for their use where the need is greatest. Because our objective is long-term sustainability, I ask you to please consider making monthly contributions for a span of five years. All contributions are meaningful, but if you want to teach a child about self-sufficiency, would you send him a single large sum of money?

Being a committed participant in the Millennium Village Project is a specific way that I choose to become grounded and accountable in living my life mission. It is one application in the larger design for my life that I have been able to realize by striving for Personal Accountability and becoming clearer about what I believe and what I can learn.

Co-creating Your Ideal Life

One of the so-called realities of growing up is that so many resign themselves to accepting what is or is not possible in their lives. Consider how many times you've been told, "Now be realistic..."

Ouch! Realistic based on what? The expectations of society? The fears of your parents who wanted to "save" you the pain of unmet expectations and failure? The capacities and capabilities of your friends and siblings? Now, being realistic can be a way of managing your expectations and making sure you are safe, but it can also be a great excuse not to risk and a marvelous story for why you should not even try in the first place.

Something that I have discovered in the past decade, working with thousands of people, is that many will not even allow themselves to dream. I find it difficult to imagine the dull ache of denying one of our greatest capacities as human beings, the ability to manifest and co-create our reality.

Have you been lowering your wants or blocking your dreams, passion, and vision? If that is still true after reading this book, I beg you to stop for the next five minutes and *not* be realistic. Don't censor your wants, dreams, and desires. Just allow yourself to be free with your thoughts and feelings so that you can answer the following questions honestly.

What do you want? What do you want to be, do and have? Live on the beach, travel the world, start a family, start a business, create a loving relationship, learn another language, become a millionaire, retire, play, teach and share what you know, express your creativity...what do you want? Allow yourself to go past the surface answers and get to what it is that you truly want.

As the picture becomes clearer and clearer, I want you to grab a piece of paper and title it "My Ideal Life." Write down your description, including where you are, how you feel, who you are with, the quality of your relationships, what you do with your time, and how you express your unique contribution to the world. I'm confident that, with your new tools and attitudes, you will no longer consider it all idle fantasy.

What you have written is your blueprint. You are now equipped to co-create your ideal life. Share it with others. Ask for support and begin taking steps toward making it a reality now!

You deserve to be, do, and have what you want in your life. One of the most powerful actions you can take to manifest your ideal life is to participate in Personal Best Level One, The Truth Revealed. With the purchase of this book, you also received as a bonus two tickets to the Truth Revealed seminar, worth almost $2,000. For more information, see Appendix 6. To activate your tickets, visit www.personalbestseminars.com

Remember, you deserve to be, do, and have what you want in your life!

The concept of Personal Accountability is a powerful, life-transforming approach. It is also a foundational tool, a choice about how you view yourself, other people, and the Universe. It allows the positive creative energy of the Universe, God, or the Source (however you choose to think of it) to flow to you and through you. And there is more: the creation of an amazing existence and your full and complete engagement in this wondrous mystery called life.

I will leave you with a thought that summarizes my beliefs about Personal Accountability. James Allen writes in his book, *As a Man Thinketh*:

> Man is made or unmade by himself. In the armory of thought, he forges the weapons by which he destroys himself. He also fashions the tools with which he builds for himself heavenly mansions of joy and strength and peace. By the right choice and true application of thought, man ascends to the divine perfection. By the abuse and wrong application of thought, he descends below the level of the beast. Between these two extremes are all the grades of character, and man is their maker and master.
>
> Of all the beautiful truths pertaining to the soul, which have been restored and brought to light in this age, none is more gladdening or fruitful of divine promise and confidence than this—that man is the master of thought, the molder of character, and the maker and shaper of condition, environment, and destiny.

It is my intention for all of you to live lives of love, joy, and contribution, whatever these terms may mean to you. I look forward to our paths crossing in one of my classrooms or in the great classroom of life.

APPENDIX 1

I have been facilitating, personal development seminars since 1989. I know how difficult it can be for people to break conditioning and let go of limiting beliefs on their own. With that in mind, I have put together the following programs, tools, and resources to support you.

Free Online Resources

www.personalbestseminars.com/free-resources.php

This page is being constantly updated with new content and resources, visit often. Some of what you will find:

- The Evolution of Personal Accountability discussion group.
- Life Mission worksheets.
- Ideal Life Worksheet and audio.
- Accountability Clues E-course, a seven-day course, delivered by e-mail, to help you stay on track applying the principles of Personal Accountability
- Personal Accountability Circles. Set up your own book study and support group to become personally accountable.
- A Time for Change, a free audio program that explores the concept of change and assists you in answering the questions necessary to create long term, meaningful change in your life.
- Pre recorded Accountability teleclasses.

APPENDIX 2

Seminars, Workshops and Teleclasses

At www.personalbestseminars.com, you'll find the Personal Freedom Program which consists of the three levels described below.

Personal Best Level One, The Truth Revealed

Level One provides the opportunity to become more aware of your mental, emotional, and behavioral patterns. You will become more conscious of the beliefs that color and shape your experience of yourself and the world around you. This increased awareness can lead to greater:

- Clarity of who you are and what you want
- Freedom of choice
- Feeling of control
- Experience of harmony

Personal Best Level Two, Pure Potential

Pure Potential is about creating quality relationships in our lives. The purpose is to create an environment that allows you to experience, accept, and share yourself openly and spontaneously. This can lead to the following experiences:

- Being the source and cause of all your life experiences
- Increasing self-confidence, self-worth, and personal power
- Recognizing parts of yourself that have been denied or not developed
- Creating congruence between who you are and the image you exert

In Pure Potential, you will begin to apply the awareness that you gained through Level One, The Truth Revealed, including the importance of keeping agreements, honesty, and openness.

Personal Best Level Three, Infinite Possibilities

Infinite Possibilities focuses on "Living It," integrating the concepts in Levels One and Two. It is this long-term integration that makes The Personal Freedom course different from most seminars.

The Focus of Infinite Possibilities:

- Accepting life as opposed to being in reaction.
- An expanded awareness. Enrolling not only in your own life, but in others' lives as well.
- Committing to living. Giving 100%, no less.
- Noticing and acknowledging the beauty around you every day.
- Nurturing self, others, and the world.
- Life purpose and mission statement.
- Having FUN in your life—enjoying the journey.
- Giving and receiving—experiencing flow and balance.

The Accountability Intensive

As I researched and developed this book, I also designed a complimentary weekend seminar called the Accountability Intensive. In this seminar, we step through the concepts presented in this book in an experiential fashion. Participants go through a series of structured activities and exercises to become personally accountable in heart, mind, and soul—a radically different experience from simply reading the book and doing a writing activity or two.

The Evolution of Personal Accountability Teleclass

You will learn to identify and step past the three levels of victimization and the energy draining they create. You'll step above the line of blame to Personal Accountability. There, you can distinguish Emotional-Response Accountability from Practical and Spiritual Accountability and experience yourself as a generator in your life and in the world. Each teleclass focuses on one of the levels of victimization/accountability. One class is also dedicated to the long term effects of victimization and being a drainer versus the long term benefits of Personal Accountability and being a generator.

The Couples Weekend

Learn how to enhance your relationship in this weekend workshop for couples in a committed primary relationship. A primary relationship can be one of life's greatest sources of joy, love, and acceptance.

The Couples Retreat

A beautiful weekend where the focus is on your partner and your relationship—no interruptions, nothing to handle, no phones ringing. It's 100 percent about you. When was the last time you concentrated on your relationship for an entire weekend? Now is the time!!

Personal Best Seminars offers many other seminars, workshops, and teleclasses. For more information, please be sure to visit the website.

APPENDIX 3

Coaching and Coach Certification Programs

www.personalbestseminars.com/coaching.php

Do you want the one-on-one personalized support that can only be provided by a Personal Coach? There are times in all of our lives when we require a little extra encouragement. Having someone in your corner who believes in you can make a difference. This support can guide you through the most challenging moments or assist you in facing and overcoming difficult circumstances. A coach can make the difference between success and stagnation.

Jumpstart Coaching

This method of coaching is perfect for you if:

- You are considering taking the Personal Freedom Program.
- You are a Personal Best grad and want one-on-one support to apply the concepts.
- You are going through a change or transition and moving into a new level in your business or personal life.
- You feel you need a boost, reminder, or swift kick in the butt!

Your Jumpstart Coaching consists of:

- Three hours of one-on-one coaching from a Personal Mastery Coach (Additional time can be added at an hourly rate.)
- The "Your Key to Balance and Achievement" online goal setting program
- The "Unlock Your Personal Best & Live It!" online audio series

Appendices

Personal Accountability Coaching

This highly flexible coaching program is formatted with your needs in mind. You and your coach will design the process to support you strategically. The fundamental objectives are:

- Reframing your blame
- Releasing the negative drain of victimization
- Creating meaning in your life
- Utilizing your recurring Victim experiences to identify your life mission
- Consciously committing and living your life mission
- Being personally accountable

APPENDIX 4

Audio Programs

You can instantly download these programs from:
www.personalbestseminars.com/online-store.php

Accountability and Expressing Love

This thirty-minute audio is a recording of Jay Fiset, President of Personal Best Seminars, speaking live at a new-thought church on the topic of allowing love. It covers the three prerequisites of allowing love and explores how, through applying the concept of Personal Accountability, you can remove the walls that may be blocking your experience of giving and receiving love freely.

Accountable Conversations

An audio series that features people who have used the principles of Personal Accountability to direct their energy, overcome challenges, and commit to their life missions.

Unlock Your Personal Best & Live It! Online Audio Series

This audio series includes twenty-plus hours of programming that follows the fundamental tenets of the Personal Freedom Program. It consists of twelve two-part audio lessons, each on a specific topic. Each lesson has an exercise to help you apply the concepts as quickly and as effectively as possible into your daily life.

In addition to the audio lessons, you also receive a workbook in which you can work through the exercise for each lesson. These aren't just more motivational audios that you listen to once and forget about. They are about rolling up your sleeves and getting to work applying the concepts to your life. That is the "Live It" part!

APPENDIX 5

www.personalbestsemianrs.com/coordinate.php

Bring Personal Accountability to your organization or community: Coordinate a Personal Accountability Event!

Keynote speech

A one-hour presentation that strikes a chord with the audience. Inspiring, entertaining and practical, it provides the audience with everything they need to reframe their blame and become Personally Accountable.

Evening Workshops

Two-hours to four-hours long, depending on your requirements. These interactive and experiential programs support participants as they actively reframe their blame, become generators, and answer the question, "How could my recurring experiences of victimization be the most important clue to my life mission?"

The Accountability Intensive Weekend

This weekend seminar by Jay Fiset, President of Personal Best Seminars, inspires and supports you as you apply the *single most significant* prerequisite to growth and development—Personal Accountability. Learn how to: (1) Release yourself and others from blame; (2) Acquire emotional freedom; (3) Expand insight into your life purpose; (4) Develop direction and focus; (5) Increase personal energy; (6) Obtain cleaner and clearer relationships; (7) Enhance capacity and willingness to risk.

Jay Fiset can custom-design programs for your business or community. He is available for private coaching and consultations. Call 1-877-806-2378 or
email: info@personalbestseminars.com

APPENDIX 6

Free Bonus Seminar

As you may have noticed, this book includes—as a bonus—two seats in the Personal Best Level One: Truth Revealed course.

Level One provides the opportunity to become more aware of your mental, emotional, and behavioral patterns. You will become more conscious of the beliefs that color and shape your experience of yourself and the world around you. This increased awareness can lead to greater:

- Clarity of who you are and what you want
- Freedom of choice
- Feeling of control
- Experience of harmony

Level One Topics

Your Relationships
- The degree to which you are willing to give and receive
- What it is within you and others that attracts you to them and them to you
- What makes you want to avoid others or makes them want to avoid you

Trust
- What you believe about trust and how it impacts your relationships

Your Dreams and Desires
- What do you really want in life?

Agreements
- The importance and value of keeping agreements you make in life
- How this affects your self esteem, your activities, your work, and your relationships

Accountability
- The extent to which you let yourself feel powerless in life by thinking that something or someone else "did it to me" or "it wasn't my fault"
- How you can experience power and control in your life by operating from the position that you create your own experiences

Abundance and Prosperity
- How you can experience more love, time, money, and freedom in your life

How You Play the "Game of Life"
- A wake up call to what you are doing and not doing to create the results you currently have

Considerations
- Identifying and addressing the excuses, limitations, and barriers that are in the way of what you want

To claim your complimentary two seats in the Personal Best Level One: Truth Revealed course, you will need the reference number located on the back inside cover of this book, at the bottom of the certificate. If there is no number shown, then you can write your number in that place. Your reference number will be one of the following four types of numbers:

- The *invoice number* if you have received an invoice for your book purchase.

- The *order number* in the confirmation email you received, if you purchased the book online.

- An *Admin number* you will receive by calling the office at 1-877-806-2378 if you purchased the book at a Personal Best event and did not receive an invoice.

- An *affiliate number* if you received the book as a gift. Please call the office if you received a gift book without an affiliate number.

When you call in to the office or go online to www.personalbestseminars.com to register for the complimentary Level One course, you will be asked which of the four types of numbers you have and what that number is.

We hope you create value in working through the book and that you or someone in your life will benefit from the complimentary Level One course. If you have any questions, please call your Personal Mastery Coach, or call the office at 1-877-806-2378.

Jay, Cory, and Wyatt enjoy an afternoon in Banff.

ABOUT THE AUTHOR

Jay Fiset is a powerful speaker, a risk-taker, and a leader who reaches his goals by assisting others to achieve theirs. He has over 20,000 hours experience conducting seminars. His company, Personal Best Seminars, is a leading seminar company that provides workshops promoting self-awareness and stimulating personal growth.

Jay enjoys living life to the fullest. He continually challenges himself and expands his comfort zone by participating in such activities as bungee jumping, sky diving, and fire-walking.

His interests include television and video production, restoring vintage sports cars, running (he completed his first marathon in Victoria in 2005), Macintosh computers, real estate investing, and learning new technology.

He is committed to personal development, conscious parenting, lifelong learning, the end of extreme poverty, community contribution, and discovery.